Creating Product Strategies

MARKETING FOR MANAGERS

This new series provides a set of workbooks focusing on key marketing techniques to help the reader develop expertise in marketing planning and management. Each title presents the central issues around each topic, including:

- a framework in which to start applying these skills;
- self-assessment exercises;
- tool kit of guidelines to improve the performance of the company or department.

Areas covered include segmentation, forecasting, customer service and marketing research. By using these workbooks the reader can analyse particular situations and develop suitable strategies in order to improve the performance of the company or department.

Already published in the series:

Auditing Your Customer Service: John Leppard and Liz Molyneux
Market Segmentation – A Step-by-step Guide to Profitable New Business: Michael J. Croft.

Creating Product Strategies

Beth Rogers

INTERNATIONAL THOMSON BUSINESS PRESS
I ⑆P An International Thomson Publishing company

London • Bonn • Boston • Johannesburg • Madrid • Melbourne • Mexico City • New York • Paris
Singapore • Tokyo • Toronto • Albany, NY • Belmont, CA • Cincinnati, OH • Detroit, MI

Creating Product Strategies

First published 1996 by International Thomson Business Press

A division of International Thomson Publishing Inc.
The ITP logo is a trademark under licence

British Library Cataloguing-in-Publication Data
A catalogue record for this book is available from the British Library

Library of Congress Cataloguing-in-publication Data
A catalogue record for this book is available from the Library of Congress

First printed 1996

Typeset in the UK by J&L Composition Ltd, Filey, North Yorkshire
Printed in the UK by Biddles Ltd, Guildford and King's Lynn

ISBN 0–415–13256–8

International Thomson
Business Press
Berkshire House
168–173 High Holborn
London WC1V 7AA
UK

International Thomson
Business Press
20 Park Plaza
14th Floor
Boston MA 02116
USA

— Contents

— *Figures*

— *Preface*

Imagination is more important than knowledge.

(Einstein)

When organisations pursue the goal of becoming customer-focused, they cannot afford to neglect their product or services. Most aspects of the marketing mix can be tweaked tactically in the short term, but 'product' requires strategic concentration. The successful introduction of new products is considered by leading business academics to be critical to the survival of companies in the late 1990s, due to higher customer expectations and the increasing pace of technological innovation.

In fact, it has always been the case that, if an organisation's product fails to meet customer needs, it is only a matter of time before the organisation fails. It is not just that companies must introduce new products, but they must also be imaginative about how they develop all product offerings to meet varied and changing customer requirements. Long-term effort is required to ensure that companies maintain a systematic and effective approach to product and service innovation which is relevant to customer expectations. There is no strategic advantage quite like having a delivered product experience which is recognised as 'best in class'.

Marketing professionals must approach the concept of product creatively and pragmatically. Lots of ideas, as well as lots of data, are required in order to develop winning product strategies.

Whilst organisations spend a lot of time and money ensuring that managers have sufficient data upon which to base practical decisions, not so much effort and investment is devoted to ensuring a plentiful supply of ideas. Creativity training is often regarded as

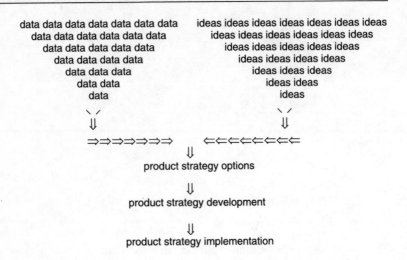

data data data data data data data   ideas ideas ideas ideas ideas ideas ideas
data data data data data data   ideas ideas ideas ideas ideas ideas
data data data data data   ideas ideas ideas ideas ideas
data data data data   ideas ideas ideas ideas
data data data   ideas ideas ideas
data data   ideas ideas
data   ideas

product strategy options

product strategy development

product strategy implementation

frivolous. Business culture has for a long time preferred scientific, rational, analytical management. This leads to a situation in which innovation happens in forced circumstances – legislative change, a technology breakthrough, a change in consumer taste, cost pressures.

Intuition, which used to be needed because of lack of information, is associated with despised 'seat of the pants' management. The truth is that the future cannot be analytically determined; statistical extrapolations fail. Speculative vision is more likely to help an organisation shape the future. If people know where they want to get to, it is easier to work out how to get there.

Without innovation, companies have retreated into niches and died. The British motorcycle industry retreated from Japanese imports in their mass markets, then in their niche markets, until they reached the point of extinction. A British pump manufacturer, faced with aggressive foreign competition in the 1980s, redesigned its products to meet the competition head on and has grown sevenfold in the last 10 years – in home and export markets. In fact, the company is now a market leader in Japan. World-class companies find new ideas to beat competitors; they have the will to thrive, not just survive.

Recent research at Cranfield into the future of marketing indicates that the accelerating pace of product innovation is a key challenge for businesses in the 1990s. As well as incremental product and service development, breakthroughs must also be sought. Therefore, businesses need to provide the right environment for the generation of ideas and, since the best breakthrough ideas are never perfect when first conceived, businesses also require the right thinking processes to convert ideas into innovation.

Ideas are not a matter of black magic, everyone in touch with an organisation can come up with ideas that might improve its performance. Quantity of ideas is as important as quality if constant innovation is a critical success factor. The challenge for any organisation is to be hungry for them, and manage the business accordingly.

ABOUT THIS BOOK

As a manager, consultant and academic I have noted the difficulty that even the most powerful companies have in encouraging and sharing ideas about developing whole products which will deliver strategic competitive advantage. In particular, departmental barriers can prevent a sum of good parts fulfilling their collective potential.

The first part of this book talks about the teams and techniques which will keep the creative raw material for new product strategy alive and kicking. Chapter 2 charts the pursuit of new product breakthroughs. Chapter 3 describes how product ideas are developed into a product 'core', and Chapter 4 clothes the core with services and intangibles. Chapter 5 demonstrates the potential for product variation to meet different aspects of need. Chapter 6 discusses the relationship of product strategy with other aspects of the marketing mix, and Chapter 7 details implementation issues.

Many of the examples and exercises in this book refer to manufactured products, but companies developing services or delivering intangible products also should be able to appreciate and apply the contents and arguments.

Consider the following shocking examp[le of bureaucratic] neglect. In 1983 it was discovered that blood [could be] heat-treated to kill the HIV virus. However, what wa[s to be done] with blood products already at transfusion centres a[nd in] refrigerators of haemophiliacs? Surely, a prime case for im[medi]ate investment in the new technology and recall of old stocks.

In France, a health official told his staff that recalling stocks of blood contaminated with HIV would have serious financial consequences. He failed to see the human consequences – the slow death of thousands of haemophiliacs from Aids. The *Wall Street Journal* quoted by Robert Wernick (1993) called it 'a crime that epitomises the darkest features of our bureaucratic age'. This health official was convicted in 1992 of distributing dangerous substances, fined £60,000 and jailed for four years. Other French health officials were found guilty of lesser charges. The relatives of the haemophiliacs affected by his decision thought the charge should have been murder. One relative is suing the French ministers concerned.

Bureaucratic neglect also affects commercial organisations, even when failure to innovate is a matter of life and death. There are a few classic cases of failure to supersede dangerous products, and there are many more of failing to supersede products which no longer delight customers.

The need for change can be easily ignored or suppressed. Psychologist Irving Janis (1971), who studied the conduct of the military and political elite running the Vietnam War, identified a phenomena he called 'groupthink'. Any member who questioned the escalation of the War was derided as soft on communism, not patriotic enough, and worse. The doubters became reluctant to express their ideas. Organisational behaviour professionals observe groupthink in many businesses. It can particularly affect product strategy. Once the product which launched a company has been successful for a long time, many careers have been devoted to it. To suggest to the managers who owe their personal prosperity to product X that it is time to plan for its succession is to remind them of their own mortality. Whether it is personal identification with the product or just short-term pursuit of dividends to please the shareholders in the here and now, companies have a tendency to transmogrify their cash cows into sacred cows.

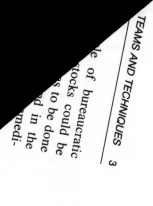

steaks.

olosi quoted in Roger van Oech, 1983)

een a product life-cycle diagram knows
start the quest for a new product before
ks. Professor Charles Handy explores the
:urve in *The Empty Raincoat* (1994). He
ip the life of people, political systems, and
products. We start, we grow, we blossom,
d we die (see Figure 1.1).
the curve if you start a new curve before the
first c   Figure 1.2).

But, before the first curve peaks, managers are feeling that
everything is going so well. Why change? So, usually, they leave
change until after the curve starts to dip (see Figure 1.3).

Wise are they who start the second curve at Point A, because
that is the Pathway through Paradox, the way to build a new
future while maintaining the present.

(Professor Charles Handy)

The only way to achieve such wisdom, is to abandon the 'one great
heave' approach to innovation, which normally, when hindsight is
applied, means 'one great panic somewhat later than we would
have liked'.

It is inevitable that innovation is required in the long term.
Evidence indicates that those organisations that embrace that
challenge can also innovate in the short term, regularly. To look
forward 10 or more years, we have to use our imagination because
there is no statistical technique that could produce anything helpful
in the quest for products to delight future markets. Setting up the
framework for meetings in which employees can use their imagination is a relatively small investment, and is likely to deliver
favourable results quickly. As Johnston concluded – a no-lose
proposition.

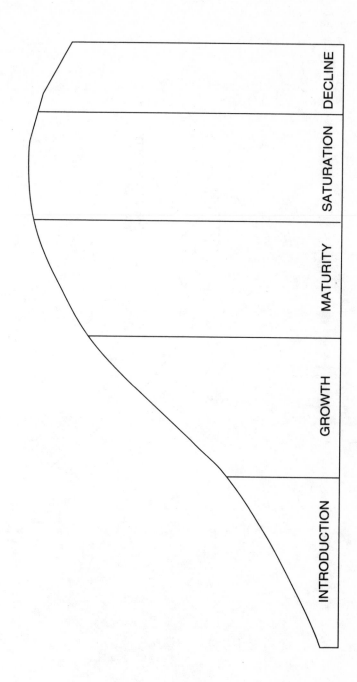

Figure 1.1 The product life-cycle

Figure 1.2 The Sigmoid curve

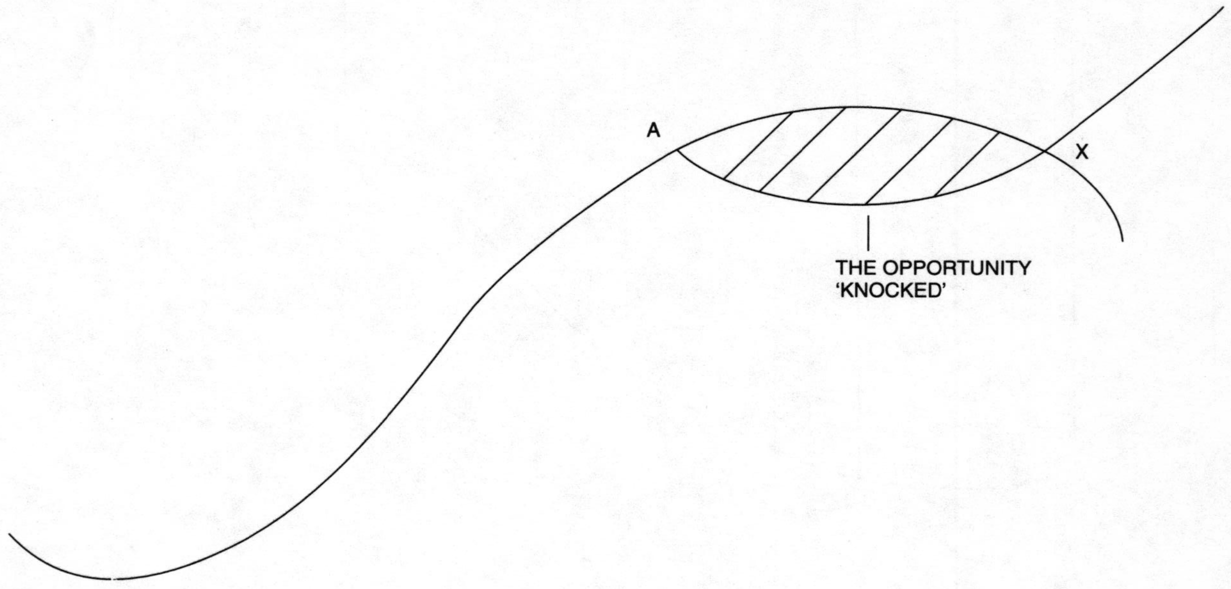

THE OPPORTUNITY
'KNOCKED'

A

X

Figure 1.3 The Sigmoid curve showing chasm of missed opportunity

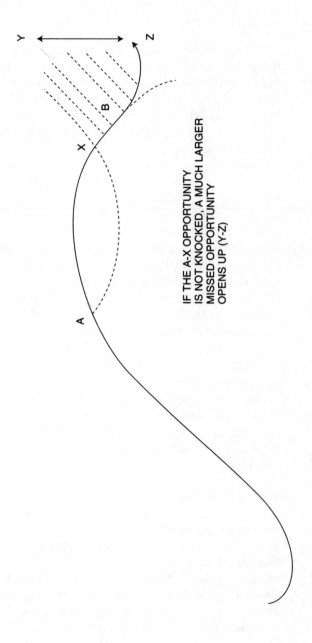

IF THE A-X OPPORTUNITY
IS NOT KNOCKED, A MUCH LARGER
MISSED OPPORTUNITY
OPENS UP (Y-Z)

WHAT IS CREATIVITY?

Creativity is the thought process by which humans bring new things to the drawing board. It is the process of idea-generation and is distinct from innovation, which is the process of converting preferred ideas into real products. Ideas are being generated in human brains all the time – the brain is constantly recalling items of disparate information and sometimes throws them together in new combinations.

Product breakthroughs are recombinations or reinterpretations of known things. For example, the inventor of the printing press had recombined his recollections of a coin punch and a wine press. Painter and decorator Mike Keenan's brother made a comment to him about the strange fact that ash given off by power stations did not burn. He wondered whether it could be mixed with paint to make a fireproof paint. He found a successful formula within a year, after trying thousands of permutations. A moment of inspiration, followed by months of perspiration, delivers progress.

Invention is also fuelled by analogy. Many significant inventions have been made by reinterpreting what happens in nature – the technology of the telephone was based on what takes place in our ears. In other cases, inventors have taken what they have learned in a hobby and applied it at work. A laboratory technician applied a principle from scuba diving to design safe packaging for sensitive computer disks. In order to come up with products which fulfil needs, inventors often derive inspiration from what the need *is like*. They seek analogies.

Example: Throat tissue – aircraft wings

A cure for some types of snoring was derived from aircraft wing technology. Surgeons from Addenbrookes Hospital in Cambridge got together with engineers from Peterhouse College. The engineers were used to the concept of thickening soft materials to reduce vibration. One of the surgeons noticed that scarring made throat tissue thicker. Scar tissue can be created by laser. By June 1994, 50 patients with snoring problems had been helped by operations involving laser scarring of throat tissue.

WHERE DO COMPANIES FIND PEOPLE WHO WILL BE CREATIVE?

> Curiosity is one of the permanent and certain characteristics of a vigorous intellect.
>
> (Samuel Johnson)

> Discovery consists of seeing what everyone has seen and thinking what nobody has thought.
>
> (Anon.)

Curiosity has been acclaimed by many researchers in the field of creativity as the characteristic trait which is singularly important to idea-generation. The creative individual is also independent, able to break out of mind-sets such as 'the way we do things around here'. He or she is optimistic, enjoys humour and likes to be humorous. The creative individual can defer judgement, take risks, use imagery, tolerate ambiguity and think impulsively. The very best of the breed will also be able to test their assumptions and be prepared to persist in seeing their ideas through to implementation. The creative individual of most value to an organisation will also have skills relevant to their activities, supported by knowledge, experience and motivation. This person will be committed to the truth, willing to root out the ways in which we limit or deceive ourselves, able to integrate reason and intuition, and willing to take responsibility.

> Off the court, most of us were oddballs by society's standards – not the kind of people who blend in with others or who tailor their personalities to match what others expect of them.
>
> (Bill Russell, a player with the Boston Celtics when they won 11 out of 13 championships)

Square, a Japanese video games company, hires anyone as long as they are inventive and competent. Some 80 per cent of the staff have come from non-technical backgrounds. Teaching, acting and playing in rock bands are fertile sources of employees for Square. Once recruited, employees are encouraged to travel in order to experience for themselves the castles, forests and caves where video games are set.

Square have found their own way of identifying employees who can deliver the originality that the company needs. However, everybody has some capacity for creativity. One psychometric test sets out to assess whether the respondent's tendency is to be wholly original, or whether they prefer to be adaptive, improving things within a given framework. Both approaches are needed. Both can be found throughout any company's current work-force. Creative thinking is not something that some people do and others cannot do. It is something all humans do to varying degrees as a way of processing information.

3M is a widely admired company today, with a reputation for innovation borne out of an episode in the 1920s. 3M was a not very special sandpaper manufacturer. A laboratory assistant was keen to research glue-covered paper which would enable cars to be painted without the paint running. His boss tried to persuade him to drop it, but he persisted and invented masking tape. His chastened boss introduced a rule that laboratory staff would be able to devote 15 per cent of their time to their own research, a rule which survives to this day and which was the enabler for other famous 3M stories like Post-it notes.

It is always advisable for recruiters to look for creative traits in job applicants, but the chances are that every organisation already has plenty of creative talent in its work-force. The next challenge is how to harvest it.

> Every individual is a marvel of unknown and unrealised possibilities.
>
> (Goethe)

A creative individual may have strengths, but they are even better in collaboration with the creative strengths of others. The next section explains how to choose creative teams.

BUILDING A CREATIVE PRODUCT DEVELOPMENT TEAM

A basketball team is a group of specialists whose performance depends on individual excellence and how they play together. All creative teams, in sport and in business must have synergy – so that collectively it is greater than the sum of its members' individual talents. Thought is best developed in dialogue with others, this overcomes incoherence and enables issues to be explored from many points of view.

Peter Senge (1990) in his work on learning organisations identified the phenomenon of business teams made up of individuals with IQs over 120 demonstrating a collective IQ of 63. It is a huge challenge to build enough capacity for learning into teams to ensure that the collective IQ exceeds individual IQs. Diversity is important, even if it involves some conflict. Great teams are not characterised by lack of conflict, but in great teams conflict becomes productive. DataQuest spent several days in team sessions to resolve a conflict between Sales/Marketing and R&D which had a 30-year history.

The first essential aspect of diversity is to build the team from different functions in the organisation. Many managers believe that the concept of multi-disciplinary teams is new. But it dates back at least to 1961, when Tom Burns described them in *The Management of Innovation*, his study of Scottish electronic companies. His research revealed that the most effective way of managing innovation projects is through co-located multi-functional teams, preferably led by the same manager from initial concept to launch.

Chrysler attributes much of its recent success to reorganising engineers, marketing people and accountants into four product-focused teams. The product development cycle has been significantly reduced, which has reduced costs. Teams also reduce the need for supervision and encourage flexibility.

A maximum of seven people on one team is recommended. However, there need be no limit to the number of teams! Rubbermaid, one of the most innovative and most admired companies in the US has set up 20 multi-disciplinary idea-generation teams, each devoted to a particular product line. Manufacturing, marketing, finance and sales are represented, as well as R&D. All employees are encouraged to come up with new product ideas. They are also accepted from suppliers, and Rubbermaid's Chief Executive says that some of the best product ideas come from customers. At Rubbermaid everyone is part of the wider team and every Rubbermaid product is being continually examined by a team to see if it can be improved or replaced with something better.

Higher team productivity is also achieved where each of the members can assume a complementary role. A team full of product champions or project managers would not be very successful. There are a number of interpretations of the need for a variety of roles in teams. For product development teams, the following roles need to be fulfilled:

- Sponsor – the sponsor is usually the manager who owns the product challenge which the team are to address, but does not have to be an active member of the team. Some teams work productively without formal leadership. If the sponsor is a participant, he or she must provide a role-model for the type of risk-taking and collaboration that they want from everybody.
- Facilitator – some teams bring in a consultant from time to time to play this role – helping the team to focus, to find out what their priorities are, to develop more ideas and to resolve conflicts.
- 'Intrapreneur'/product champion – the champion will have the drive to promote the output of the team across the company.
- Inventor – the inventor comes to the team with a reputation for offering large quantities of ideas and plenty of originality to stimulate others.
- Project manager – the project manager likes to make sure that things happen according to schedule and will make sure the team keeps functioning effectively.
- Coach – the coach will be concerned with morale and making sure everyone is contributing.
- Detective – the detective will search for information or other resources as and when the team needs it.
- Recorder – someone has to keep track of what the team is doing, but the facilitator must also make sure that they have the opportunity to contribute.

Roles need not necessarily be confined to one person. Some will need to be shared. Some groups rotate the facilitator role. Some aspects of the project manager role, such as timekeeping, ought to be important to everybody. All team members are likely to get involved in searching for information or resources at some time. Also, the purpose of using the idea generation exercises which will be introduced later in this chapter is to ensure that everybody can have a go at the inventor role. The team may wish to assign a recorder for each meeting and a project manager/progress chaser for between meetings.

The final aspect of diversity which helps the productivity of the team is a variety of social perspectives. Any large company will have employees of different ages, from different regions, with different social and family backgrounds. Global companies will almost certainly want a world-wide cultural mix in their top teams. An organisation in a small town might not be able to find a cosmopolitan mix, but the important criterion is to ensure hetero-geneity, that each team member will have a different way of looking at the product development challenge. The other impor-tant criterion is that they are positive thinkers who will be asking themselves what they can do for the team and for the team's challenge.

DEVELOPING A CREATIVE PRODUCT TEAM

Having built a team, the next challenge is to develop it. As illustrated by Peter Senge (1990), a team of performers may not necessarily turn out to be a performing team. In order to develop synergy in a team, it is first advisable to evaluate how the team operates from a standing start. Many project management consult-ants use an exercise called the egg game to assess a team's strengths and weaknesses. It is most effective when a number of teams take part, then comparisons can be made and experiences exchanged when the exercise is over.

EXERCISE   THE EGG GAME

Provide each team with an egg, or several! Their challenge is to design a wrapping which will protect it from at least a 12-foot (four metres) drop. The team will have a time limit of two hours and a cost limit, which is at the facilitator's discretion. Having designed and made their solution in those two hours, observed periodically by the facilitator/s, they will present their solution and it will be tested.

In de-briefing each team, the facilitator will be able to explain what strengths they can exploit and what weaknesses they must work on. Perhaps they did not generate enough ideas, or failed to criticise constructively those they had. Perhaps time management or cost management were sloppy. The following checklist of performance criteria show what is important for the team's success.

- Quantity of ideas
- Quality of evaluation of ideas
- Feasibility of implementation plan
- Allocation of tasks
- Pragmatic approach
- Inspired approach
- Time management
- Cost management
- Focus on required result
- Mutual encouragement
- Mutual constructive criticism
- Social interaction

Teams are supposed to go through four stages of development, so it is no disaster if a product development team is not achieving synergy on day 1; you have to break a few eggs to make an omelette! A typical team goes through a period of forming, when they get to know each other. The next period is called storming, when problems are flushed out. It is followed by norm-

Figure 1.4 The team development cycle

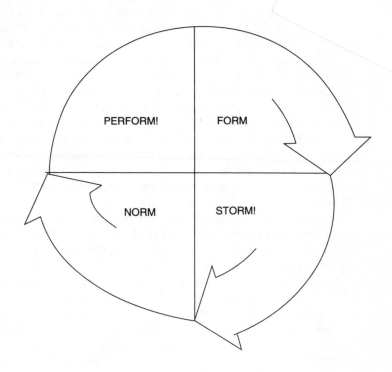

ing, a period of meeting expectations, a prelude to performing –
when synergy flows and flows.

WHAT SORT OF SUPPORTING FRAMEWORK DOES THE TEAM NEED?

It is in everybody's interests to get to the performing stage as
quickly as possible. The first thing a team needs in order to
perform is a big-game atmosphere. The Apollo space mission
inspired average groups to excel, a war effort has the same
effect. A new product project is rarely a case of '20 minutes to

save the universe', but the team needs to believe that there is something at stake. Their end result must be important.

Independence is another known success factor. It is hard for a company to develop new products whilst promoting old ones. Usually the needs of the future will give way to the imperatives of the present. Some companies completely sub-contract research and development to specialist companies, such as Craymer Inventions Ltd., a small team of seven who have won international awards. Certainly, new product teams, whether internal or external, must be free from the company's cultural pressures. In the late 1980s, as recession loomed in the UK, Midland Bank's Project Raincloud team isolated themselves from the bureaucracy and the day-to-day struggles of the bank to think about the future of banking; they developed the concept of a telebanking subsidiary which was an instant success.

Although inspiring goals and independence are vital, new product teams do need some practical support from the parent organisation. Feedback and reward are appreciated. They will also need resources, primarily information.

Another aspect of the support framework operates at a micro level. Each time the team meets, the participants need to feel the flow of progress. Whilst the product sponsor may be responsible for macro-level inspiration, it is the role of the team leader/ facilitator to pay close attention to the team's day-to-day effectiveness. As in football, the team will only succeed if there is genuine team spirit. An inherent appreciation of who is in the best position to score the goal looks fantastic on the pitch – it actually takes hours and hours of practice. New product teams may need to set aside hours of practice before they inherently understand who can do what to the best advantage of the team effort. All of the exercises in this book are suitable for practice sessions. Practice time must encompass the freedom to treat mistakes as stepping-stones. On flights between earth and the moon, Apollo spaceships were off course more than 90 per cent of the time. The crew had to repeatedly correct the trajectory, but it did not impede the overall success of the mission.

Team spirit thrives on trust. In order to build up the sort of trust which tolerates error and heresy and can constructively deal with conflict, there are problems inherent in human interaction that the team needs to avoid. Lack of clarity is a major frustration in meetings. If objectives are unclear, expectations will also be unclear and participants' attention will wander. Issues may remain unresolved and discussion topics may feel incomplete. The right level of information is important. If there is insufficient, that will worry people; if there is too much, most team members will fail to absorb it and others might manipulate it. The team will also need to avoid destructive behaviour in the group, such as talking at the same time, personal attacks and win/lose attitudes, for example.

Summary: Problems to avoid

- Unclear objectives
- Unclear expectations
- Too little information
- Information overload
- Manipulation
- Repetition
- Straying
- Unresolved issues
- Failing to complete a topic
- Talking at the same time
- Personal attacks
- Win/lose attitudes
- Insufficient preparation
- Insufficient follow-up

The following checklists should also be helpful in avoiding these pitfalls. The first addresses the challenges of the facilitator, the second is about the responsibilities of all participants.

RUNNING A NEW PRODUCT DEVELOPMENT TEAM MEETING

(Chair/facilitator's responsibilities:)

1 Preparing for the meeting

- Circulate an agenda a week in advance
- Be specific about the topic

- Offer a pithy or wise quote and an analogy
- Remind participants what is expected of them
- Remind participants of any background data they should review before coming to the meeting

2 In the meeting

Physical requirements

- Plenty of flip chart paper
- Easel at a comfortable height
- A means of sticking paper up around the room
- Big felt tip pens – lots of colours
- Desks in a horseshoe shape
- Enough chairs and elbow room for all participants
- Paper and pencil for all participants
- Facilities for sub-groups
- Ensure the room has enough light, warmth, air etc.

Procedure

- Reiterate the purpose of the meeting
- Team up those who have done their homework with those who have not
- Allow a few minutes discussion
- Start the appropriate exercise
- Put up ideas where everyone can see them
- Ensure regular breaks
- Ensure large break between idea generation and evaluation
- Do not allow sessions to overrun

3 After the meeting

- Circulate output from meeting as soon as possible and check consensus

product teams do not have to be actors, but understanding the likely reactions of others is an important aspect of imagination. The last creativity technique described involves the search for analogies – finding out what the challenge resembles in nature, folklore or other environments.

Why-Why?

The first law of creativity is to keep asking questions. In the early stages of any quest for new products, 'why?' will be the most important. Often the first exercise for the team is to establish why their organisation is in the business it is in.

> As a manager of a car company, I must be able to ask why we build cars. Only if I accept the meaning of this product for our society can I be convincing as a manager.
>   (Daniel Goeudevert, Deputy Chairman of Volkswagen AG)

The Fishbone diagram is a means of mapping many possible answers to a 'why' question, so that all the issues connected with the product challenge in hand can be flushed out.

Why do we need new products? Because of changing customer tastes, new technology, new legislation, etc.

Every 'because' must be countered with another 'why?', until every avenue of possibility has been explored and mapped.

Why do we need to improve service?

Asking why is very important in identifying root causes of difficulty in your product strategy.

Reversal

If it is difficult to see the 'because', look at the complete opposite of the situation. 'Reversal technique' is used quite widely by academics. Some of our assumptions about the way things are done are so ingrained that we do not even recognise them as assumptions, we believe that they are given truths. Systematically

Figure 1.5 Fishbone diagram 1

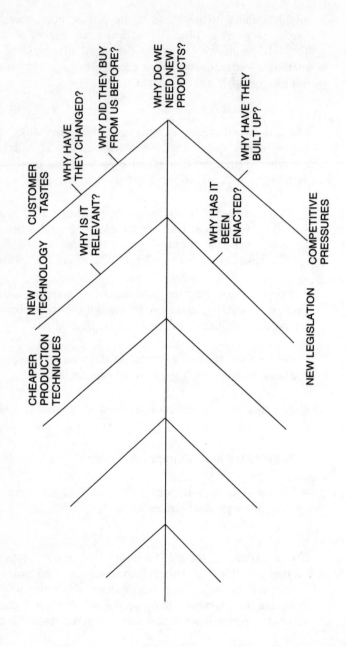

Figure 1.6 Fishbone diagram 2

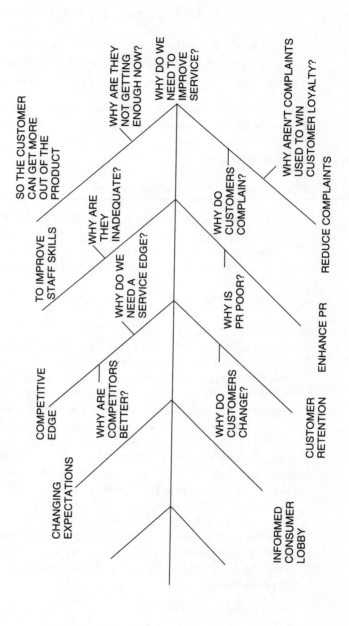

reversing them helps to break down that hierarchy of learned truths.

Adrian Furnham (in the *Financial Times*, 6/7/94), a professor of psychology, uses the example of reversing management philosophies:

- Management by walking about – management by hiding away
- Quality circles – shoddy squares
- Empowerment – disempowerment
- Delayering – relayering
- Management by objective – management without objectives
- Job enrichment – job impoverishment

If the reversal of something is absurd, it helps us to trace value in the original proposal. So, for example, if it is difficult for your team to see why a product should be re-engineered to reduce costs, use a Fishbone diagram showing the exact opposite:

Why re-engineer the product to increase costs?

Avoiding expressing judgement

It is actually impossible not to react to ideas – it is human nature to respond emotionally to ideas. However, we can avoid expressing a premature judgement. Research into the popularity of brainstorming as a creativity technique suggests that the large quantity of unusable ideas put forward creates the space in which better ideas can develop. Managers and professionals will be familiar with the impromptu 'brainstorm'. Members of the group call out ideas, any ideas, about the new product challenge. A quick-fire pace is encouraged by the facilitator, and a huge list of ideas is accumulated in 20-30 minutes. It has been discovered that the majority of breakthrough ideas emerge in the later stages of the exercise. By that time, a large number of unworkable options have been put forward – they are given equal status by the controller of the meeting, and no judgement has been expressed by anyone. They are there to be used by everyone in the team as stepping-stones to workable ideas.

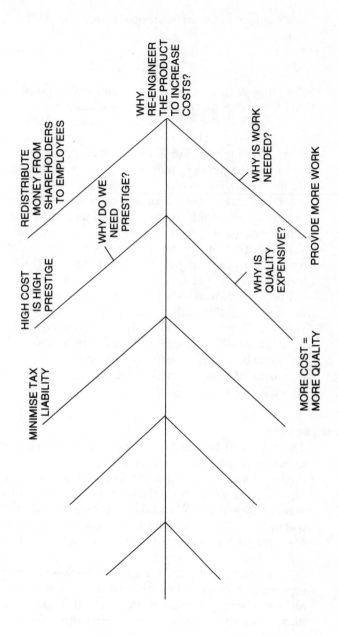

Figure 1.7 Fishbone and reversal

> Criticism often takes from the tree caterpillars and blossom together.
>
> (Jean-Paul Sartre)

The truth is that we all have parameters of given 'truths' within which we like to run our lives, and life would be unbearable if every one of those truths were subject to daily change. For example, we would soon be stressed out if our route to work every morning were subject to constant diversions.

Unfortunately, the parameters in which we have learned to live our lives are very narrow. An Aboriginal witch doctor can make a member of their tribe die of fear by pointing a bone at them, and despite all our sophistication, many of us in modern societies have some remnant of deep fear of judgement. In order to defend ourselves from it, we are often quick to judge others. There is a time and a place for judgement, but it is not the early stages of idea-generation. Encouraging people to ask why, and to challenge existing norms, will only work if they are not immediately judged for doing so. Suspending judgement and applying an 'I'm OK, you're OK' approach is not only more productive, it is much more pleasant for all concerned. Ideas are very personal, and when they are quickly judged, creativity can wither and die. Sometimes, criticisms of ideas are accidental, careless. Sometimes they constitute harassment.

Killer phrases

The team will benefit from working through what sort of judgements the team members are trying to avoid.

One of my clients told me about a manager he had reported to in his early career. Every time he came forward with an idea, the manager would say 'We tried that. It didn't work.' Even if the idea had been tried and found wanting many years previously, as far as the manager was concerned, that was reason enough for it not to be reconsidered.

'We tried it, it didn't work' is a classic 'killer phrase'. It represents a quick judgement and a death sentence for the idea and the owner's inclination to bring other ideas forward. Killer phrases are surprisingly common. Here are some more examples:

- Nobody likes a smart alec!
- Steady on – thinking can be dangerous!
- So what else is new?
- Don't waste your time trying to change things.
- It's just not the done thing!
- If you're so clever, why aren't you running the company?
- Think through the implications of this.
- Ask a stupid question and you get a stupid answer.
- If you don't like the way things are, you know where the door is.
- That's a crazy idea.
- It is too hard to administer.
- Write a report for me.
- The boss won't like it.

EXERCISE   PREVENTING KILLER PHRASES

The first step in avoiding such judgement is to be aware of it. Many facilitators of brainstorming meetings *ask their participants to exorcise their judgement beforehand by writing down all the judgemental phrases they can think of and then symbolically tear up the list.* Others issue cards, red on one side and green on the other. Whilst the idea-generation session is positive, participants display the green side. If anyone wades in with judgement, they are shown the red side.

Challenging norms through role-play

Creativity researcher B. V. Mattimore (quoted in Grossman, 1994) has demonstrated that new ideas can be generated when team members assume roles, especially superhuman roles such as Superman, Flash Gordon or Batman. At the very least, participants should practise playing the role of mortal superachievers.

Progress comes from the unreasonable man.

(George Bernard Shaw)

> If Job could challenge God's fairness . . . how much more hope
> for those seeking to challenge the far less awesome interests that
> defend corporate orthodoxy.
>
> (Professor Gary Hamel, London Business School)

Researchers who have studied superachievers, in business and in history, tell us that these people are bored by logic, but inspired by vision, more driven by emotion than analysis. And they break rules. Copernicus and Galileo committed heresy against the all-powerful medieval church by pointing out that the earth moves round the sun. Einstein and Pasteur were considered dangerously deviant. Edison's light bulb was denounced as a hoax. The Wright Brothers were ignored. Beethoven challenged the way music was supposed to be written.

Even today, people who claim to be onto a challenging discovery are often dismissed as cranks or treated as subversive heretics. The BBC recently screened a series about living scientists who have been ostracised by the scientific establishment for pursuing unusual lines of research. Should the Director of Research at the University of Paris have lost his job because he wanted to research the electro-magnetic properties of water? Should a Nobel prize winner have had to wait 20 years for his theories about the health-giving properties of high doses of Vitamin C to be taken seriously? Is it wrong to challenge Newtonian physics, the theory of DNA or psychoanalysis? As for Robert John's theories about machines playing up when their operators are under stress – can they be dismissed when so many people can identify with his premise? (My laser printer is a perfect case in point!)

Ideas are being suppressed all around us, not just by military dictatorships but by academic and commercial elites. It is especially difficult to understand why heretical inventors are shunned, since their claims are bound to be proven predominantly valid or invalid the more they are researched and tested. *Progress cannot be made by continuing research merely within the tramlines of existing knowledge.* New discoveries will overturn previously accepted truths. Creative people look forward to such events as exciting, they do not put up a barricade of denial.

EXERCISE   ROLE-PLAY + 'SO WHAT?'

Team members may assume the role of their favourite super-achiever, and practise with relevant and irrelevant 'so what?' scenarios:

- So what if Britons woke up tomorrow morning without a monarchy? Remember that recently Berliners woke up without a Wall dividing them. So what if Americans woke up tomorrow morning without Wall Street?
- So what if customers are concerned about pollution?
- So what if athletics is corrupt?
- So what if competition is forcing down the price of product X?
- So what if pandas became extinct?
- So what if we don't get a quality registration?

Note: If any team members have particular difficulty with role-play, the facilitator might help them by introducing glove puppets, so that they can role-play through the puppet.

Throughout the process of challenging norms, the application of humour will make the job easier. Humour provides a low-risk approach to slaughtering sacred cows. In the corridors and by the coffee machines, the gap between company rhetoric and the reality that employees experience is a fertile source of satirical comment. That spirit of subversion has to be encouraged in the product development team. David Kearns (quoted by Jean-Louis Barsoux in the *Financial Times*, 20/1/95) explained the role of humour in Rank Xerox's change teams:

This fooling around and digressive talk built an *ésprit de corps*.

He also said that it helped to alleviate stress.

EXERCISE   COMIC RECOMBINATIONS

In two days' casual television viewing, I noticed the following recombinations being used by comedians. What ideas or
sketches can the team make from:

- Welsh/hip-hop
- Chinese/Elvis
- Politician/pop singer
- Meteorologist/impressionist painting
- Queen/supermarket checkout

Seeking analogies

A foreman at a Californian thermodynamics plant explained why
the technicians who maintained the plant's delicate equipment had
the lowest turnover rate and highest performance, despite the
routine and repetitive nature of the work. They wear surgeon's
smocks; it was an analogy he drew with his son's work as a heart
surgeon: 'We take care of these pipes the way a doctor takes care
of a patient's heart.'

Just as plant operators can improve their job satisfaction by
seeing themselves as doctors, doctors can help their patients by
exploring the similarities between human organs and fruit. They
train for keyhole surgery on hernias and gall bladders using
oranges.

Guidelines for seeking analogies

- First of all, assume all things are possible. After all, flying for-
  tresses were once an inventor's 'castles in the air'.
- Remember that the search is for a new way of looking at something, not a solution.
- Analogy can accommodate imprecision. Respect your own half-
  formed ideas.
- Entertain the impossible or unspeakable and use humour (if
  necessary) to introduce it.
- Make the familiar strange and the strange familiar.

■ Listen to the analogies of others and see if you can build on them.

SUMMARY OF CHAPTER 1

■ Asking why is very fundamental, and a prerequisite to working out how.
■ Reversing and re-reversing situations can provide new insights.
■ During idea-generation workshops, team members should avoid expressing judgement and letting slip 'killer phrases'.
■ Role-playing and humour can help team members to challenge norms.
■ There are very few new things under the sun. Seeking an analogy for a situation can reveal that there is already a solution to the challenge in hand.

2 *Working for new product breakthroughs*

New product breakthroughs are relatively rare, but it is natural to aspire to them. The first part of this chapter describes a technique designed to encourage a high volume of abstract new product ideas from the team. Product-led innovation has played an important role in history. Some of the greatest new products have been delivered to the world as a result of pure, rather than applied research. Penicillin was discovered by accident and was not widely used until the Second World War accelerated its manufacture.

Recent examples include the classic Post-it notes, which have had a major impact on the office stationery cupboard. The concept was developed as part of 3M's programme of allowing staff 15 per cent of their time for their own experimentation. Aspartame, the sweetener more commonly known by its brand name 'Canderel', was also discovered by accident.

Nevertheless, pure research is an expensive luxury. Little is said about the ideas that get discarded on the way to the 'Big Idea', but academics estimate that the ratio of raw ideas to implementable ideas is at least 60:1. It is often the 'intermediate impossible' which has the greatest innovative potential, and is therefore most costly and risky to develop. It takes pharmaceutical companies many years to recoup the huge research investment in new drugs.

The second part of this chapter explores examples of needs-based innovation. Day to day, an organisation devoted to innovation, such as Rubbermaid, wll be encouraging and collecting ideas from employees, customers and suppliers – ideas which identify needs or potential solutions. Additional new product development team activity is also pursued.

Needs-based innovation can provide meaningful, if not necessarily dramatic, product breakthroughs. When the team is working from a need, rather than in the abstract, their creative effort can be accompanied by objective research of external sources of ideas. This chapter discusses those external sources as well as providing an exercise to provoke ideas from the product development team.

ABSTRACT GENERATION OF NEW PRODUCT IDEAS

Most new product ideas are recombinations of known things. The inventor of the printing press said that he had combined the concept of a wine press and the concept of a coin punch to come up with his revolutionary product. In order to come up with new product ideas, remembering that quantity is the first priority, the product development team can work on forced recombinations. This exercise should be familiar, as it is often used by primary school teachers. To ask children to write a story or draw a picture involving apparently unrelated objects, such as a dragon, a box and an umbrella, develops their imagination as much as their writing or drawing skills.

The procedure is quite simple. To start off with the team brainstorms two lists of objects – 15 in each would be sufficient. The facilitator then pairs items at random and asks teams of two to come up with ways in which each pair might be linked to create something useful. Examples are shown following the exercise.

EXERCISE   FORCED RECOMBINATIONS

Summary

- Brainstorm two lists of objects
- Pair items at random
- Describe ways in which the pairs can be linked as products

EXAMPLE   FORCED RECOMBINATION 1

List A	List B
Slug	Case
Water	Cushion
Door	Bell
Tile	Shoe
Tank	Blanket
Daffodil	Car
Glass	Radiator
Seat	Cupboard
Bag	Rose
Washing line	Switch
Tree	Wall
Streetlight	Bus stop
Calendar	Toilet
File	Window

EXAMPLE   FORCED RECOMBINATION 2

Selection	Solutions
Slug and car	Apply the clinging power of a slug to tyre technology to prevent skidding
	Produce cars that glide along the road
	Use cars to kill slugs
Daffodil and blanket	Gardeners use plastic sheeting to warm the earth to encourage early plant growth
	Colourfully patterned blankets to cheer up hospital patients
	Scented blankets – aromatherapy
Streetlight and radiator	Underground heating linked to the lighting system could help to keep footpaths free of snow and ice
	Buy a radiator – sponsor a streetlight
	Recycle old radiators for street furniture
Sword and cushion	Already been used as an advertising image – smooth shave
	Design a special blade to remove pet hair from cushions
	Flexible, guarded cutting edges for dressmakers or carpenters

Recombinations work in practice. Anil Vora is a Hong-Kong-based entrepreneur who manufactures simple new product ideas for the consumer market. Many of these are recombinations, such as a combined toothbrush and dental flosser, and a pen incorporating a perfume spray. Others display applications of simple technology from other products to consumer products, such as his vented umbrellas which do not blow inside out, and the windless baby feeding bottle, which prevents the baby from sucking air by means of a simple valve.

Many companies successfully use recombinations to develop their product line, but concentrate their item lists around their existing product range. Rubbermaid have a number of recombination options, for example, in order to save space in the garage you can buy a Rubbermaid stepping stool which doubles up as a tool box.

Some teams may prefer to follow this concentrated route. However, practice with abstract examples is always recommended first. It is fun, it does not have to take very long and it is an excellent exercise for the imagination. It is easier to practise creative convergent thinking having previously indulged in complete divergence.

NEEDS-BASED SOLUTION GENERATION

Inventing a product and then looking for a need to fulfil has had its outstanding successes, but most successful entrepreneurs have identified a need and set out to meet it in a very systematic way. There are different types of need in the market, each requiring a different product development approach.

Specific needs

Specific needs can be described very simply, they are well understood and apply to a great number of people. For example, I heard the brand manager of a new washing powder describe the need to which it was addressed very bluntly: 'your clothes smell, our product can do something about it!'

Glue is a household staple because so many people have a need to stick things together; people buy drills because they have a need to make holes; and people buy cars because they have a need to get from A to B. Specific needs are gratifying for the inventor to fulfil as they require a finite commodity product in response, and can be the short-cut to a fortune.

The search for more and better solutions to specific needs is always on. Sony, among others, have taken laser technology out of the factory and into the home to produce better music systems. Microchip technology has been applied to household appliances to achieve better quality, and all kinds of chemicals are mixed and remixed in pursuit of the best washing powder. In the realm of personal transport, Hydro-Quebec has developed a hybrid electric car technology designed to reduce emissions and increase energy efficiency. Leaping further into the future, Californian Paul Moller has designed a flying car and a prototype has been produced.

It is possible to come across specific needs which are not properly addressed, usually in emerging market segments. Most of the developed world expects large increases in the number of elderly consumers and 'grey power' during the next 30 years. Recent prime examples of new products to address specific needs have been designed for this huge and growing market.

In 1978, Roy Parker, a UK businessman who was making award-winning boat fittings was challenged by a dinner party

Figure 2.1 Analysis of type of need

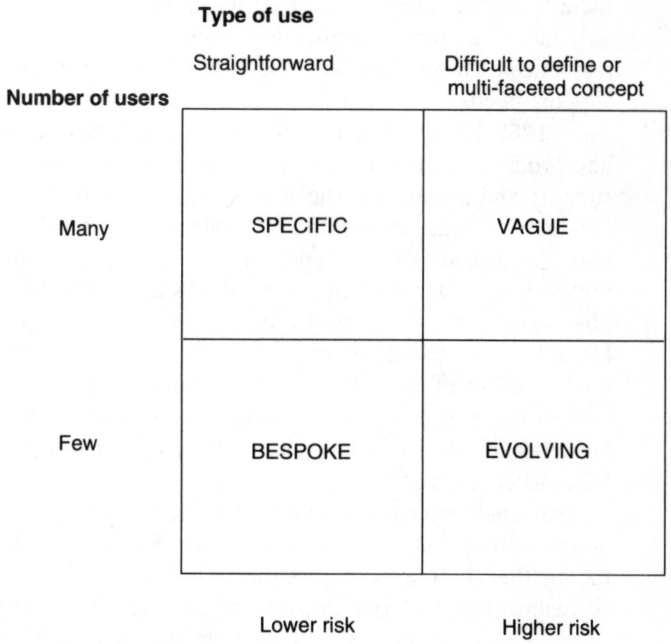

	Type of use	
Number of users	Straightforward	Difficult to define or multi-faceted concept
Many	SPECIFIC	VAGUE
Few	BESPOKE	EVOLVING
	Lower risk	Higher risk

guest to design a way of lifting old people into baths. Mr Parker worked out that lifting was not the answer, the best way of washing someone with limited mobility was to throw water at them. He designed a way of doing that with dignity. His tipping orthopaedic bath was the award-winning foundation product for a £21 million export-oriented business (source: *The Director*, August 1994).

Bespoke needs

There are needs which are quite straightforward, but because they are required by only a few individuals or organisations, the solution can be tailored for each customer or group of customers. The addition or exclusion of features for each customisation serves also to develop the product concept as a whole. The ideal example of bespoke needs is computer services. A company may offer a consistent set of skills and software tools to fulfil customers' needs to network their computers together in order to ensure information can pass seamlessly around their organisation. Nevertheless, each contract will be different because no two companies will have the same number and configuration of computers and resident software. The same is true of other information system support needs.

In 1989 Hilary Warren set up Shamrock Marketing to pursue her product idea – a customer information system that would support and streamline the marketing efforts of large companies conducting industry-to-industry sales. She developed the idea partly as a result of her experience managing the Central Marketing Services Department of NCR UK and also through careful observation of information technology trends. Leaps in usage of IT had tended to follow recessions. She correctly anticipated that the recession of the 1990s would trigger the application of information systems to reduce escalating sales and marketing costs in large organisations. Hilary also backed up her intuition with careful market research.

Shamrock's system has proved particularly popular with capital goods companies, utilities companies and government agencies facing the challenge of privatisation. Each sale is a package of software, technical and consultancy services. The software and the services can be tailored to each customer's requirements. The company is extremely successful and is continuously improving the software and expanding the services offered around the core software function.

A set of generic tools and skills, tailored to each customer's requirements, also characterises cleaning services, catering, building and decorating. Many industry-to-industry products and services fulfil bespoke needs, but bespoke needs also exert influence in some consumer industries, such as fashion.

'Off-the-peg' has the lion's share of the fashion industry, but the majority of the population are not a standard shape. Specialist shops cater for particularly tall men and large women, and many chain stores have specialist sections for 'petite'. More exclusive stores offer alteration services. The very richest consumers of fashion can employ top designers to manufacture one-off items of clothing for them.

Vague needs

Vague needs are not easy to describe and are very difficult to research. They are the needs which we hint at in our behaviour, but do not express. They are the needs we know are there, but cannot define or pin down because the need is so variable. They are also the needs which arise from new situations presenting unacceptable alternatives – situations where the decision-makers know what they do not want but have not yet been presented with what they do want. The products which are invented to fulfil vague needs rely very much on inspiration and intuition.

Market researchers have a considerable challenge in trying to pin down whether consumers' buying intentions will actually be borne out in buying behaviour. The same is true of opinion polls; polled voting intentions are not always carried through into election results. Researchers would not aspire to picking up aspects of behaviour which only hint at a need, but entrepreneurs have to have the courage to develop products in response to hints of need.

'I knew from my own experience at home that young people cannot seem to live without music . . . . I remembered that one time when my daughter came home from a trip she ran upstairs before even greeting her mother and first put a cassette into her stereo.'

Akio Morita of Sony (1987) describes the inspiration behind the Sony Walkman. He says that nobody liked the idea, he could not even convince his own project team. His accountants did not like Morita's insistence that the product should be cheap enough for young people's pockets and Sony's marketers believed that it would not sell. Young people were not overtly expressing the need for a portable personal stereo, but Morita had spotted the unexpressed, undefined need. He asserts that market research could not have revealed that the Sony Walkman would be successful. Intuition and courage were required to develop the small item which changed the music listening habits of millions of people.

Evolving needs

There are plenty of examples of the difficulties involved in meeting evolving needs. Innovative engineering projects, such as the Anglo-French supersonic airliner Concorde, are renowned for running over time and over budget, disappointing investors, governments and potential customers. Every systems integration and business process redesign project being undertaken in companies today is subject to similar high-risk factors relative to the size of the organisation. The degree of newness and change, the length of time to complete and the amount of money involved make such projects difficult to manage. In addition, because of the passage of time, requirements change, and the environment in which the project is executed also changes. From ancient Egyptian Imhotep's stepped pyramid at Memphis to the 1994 refit of the cruise liner the *QE2*, unforeseen complications involving anything from the forces of nature to the natural frailty of future predictions affect the whole effort.

Nevertheless, there would have been no progress without the first Roman road, the first medieval flying buttress, the first broad-gauge railway, the first desalination plant or the first personal computer. One of the greatest historical achievements was the first manned moon landing. In 1961, President John F. Kennedy announced the Apollo programme to put a man on the moon by the end of the decade. The Apollo II mission landed a man on the moon in 1969. This was an amazing and inspiring success.

The technological feat of a manned moon landing was an end in itself. There was faith that, through this project, the US would achieve technology breakthroughs which would have valid military and (later) industrial applications. There was also the great intangible, that the project would deliver tremendous prestige to the United States and pride to all Americans.

At the time, the USA was a very rich nation, able to invest billions of dollars in the project, so problems with curtailed budgets and minimum returns on investment were never going to arise. Nevertheless, it was helpful, in terms of maintaining public support for such an expensive programme, that there were so many milestones to cheer. There were 17 Apollo missions in total, including six follow-up missions after the historic breakthrough.

The choice among competing techniques for achieving a moon landing and return was not made until extensive research had been carried out. This homework in advance was another success factor. It is also noteworthy that the programme was not excessively delayed by its catastrophes. Finally, and perhaps decisively, people working on the Apollo programme were inspired by the vision. Psychologists reported that teams with performance ratings in NASA's bottom 50 per cent leapt into the top 15 per cent when they were doing something for the moon programme.

From the Apollo example, we can extrapolate the following quick checklist for successful innovation to meet evolving needs:

- Is the proposed product worthwhile as a feat in its own right?
- Are spin-off benefits likely? Will it deliver prestige to those involved?
- Does the customer have a realistic appreciation of the amount of money and time involved? Even if money is no object, there should be frequent milestones to please budget holders.
- Will the customer pay for sufficient research in advance of commencement of work?
- Does the customer understand the likelihood of problems and mistakes?
- Are contingency plans in place in the event of problems occurring?
- Do the people involved with the project feel inspired by the challenge?

EXERCISE   FINDING SOLUTIONS – A NEEDS ANALYSIS CHECKLIST

Circle the answers and scores which relate to the need you are trying to fulfil			
Question	Answer	X score	Y score
Is the need to be fulfilled easy to define?	Yes	Low	
	No	High	
How many potential purchasers have this need?	Millions+		High
	Few		Low
How much service will be required?	Much		Low
	Little		High
How important are intangible benefits, such as prestige?	Very imp.	High	
	Not imp.	Low	
Is there already a way of fulfilling this need?	Yes	Low	
	No	High	
How quickly can the need be gratified?	Quickly		High
	Slowly		Low

The purpose of completing the questionnaire is to establish in advance the parameters for product development. To avoid spurious accuracy, only general Low/High indicators have been used.

■ If you have 2 or more Low X scores and 2 or more Low Y scores, the need you are trying to fulfil is most likely to be BESPOKE
■ If you have 2 or more High X scores and 2 or more High Y scores, the need you are trying to fulfil is most likely to be VAGUE

Figure 2.2 Analysis of product development approach

Type of use

	Straight forward	Difficult to define or multi-faceted concept
Number of users Many	SPECIFIC Quality and design Market research External sources	VAGUE Quality and design Try and buy Intangibles important
 Few	BESPOKE Services Skills-service providers	EVOLVING Powerful concept Skills-service providers Deliver intangibles Manage risk
	Lower risk	Higher risk

Key: SPECIFIC
The quality and design of the product are very important as it will be sold 'as-is'. It will be possible to research product requirements in advance and during development. It may also be quite easy to find solutions from external sources.

VAGUE
The quality and design of the product which will fulfil vague needs are also very important as it will be sold 'as-is'. However, it will be very difficult to research product requirements in advance, therefore considerable attention will have to be paid at product launch to getting consumers to try out the product.

BESPOKE
The product must be accompanied from Day 1 by skilled people providing services individual to each user or group of users. Development of the core will assume relatively less importance than the development of tailoring services.

EVOLVING
The product must have value as a concept, and deliver intangible benefits as a concept. Motivated, skilled people providing services individual to each user or group of users will be required. Careful attention to risk assessment and contingency planning will be vital.

- If you have 2 or more Low X scores and 2 or more High Y scores, the need you are trying to fulfil is most likely to be SPECIFIC
- If you have 2 or more High X scores and 2 or more Low Y scores, the need you are trying to fulfil is most likely to be EVOLVING

FINDING SOLUTIONS – EXTERNAL SOURCES

A project team which has identified a need and wishes expediently to fulfil it, should first seek a solution from outside the company. An inventor with a creative solution does not always rush off and develop a successful business. Enterprise and reward are not universally linked in this way, and a lot of good ideas never reach fruition.

James Dyson, the British inventor of a new vacuum cleaner, showed his first breakthrough design to established manufacturers in the UK. They rejected it. He licensed the design to a Japanese company and subsequent designs to American companies. He used the income from these licences to set up on his own in the UK to compete with those companies who had failed to take up his first design.

So, companies who do not work with inventors may regret it in the long term. They should be proactively seeking out inventors! Once it is understood what need is to be fulfilled, members of the group can check to see if an invention is already meeting it.

A direct source of help in the search for unexploited inventions is the local Patent Office. Most Patent Offices now have computer-based records and can offer a (probably chargeable) global search, as an exchange service has been set up between patent libraries around the world. The British Library has a collection of 34 million patents on CD-ROM.

Additional desk research could be conducted via computer networks such as the Internet. Many computer network services offer data-base coverage of academic and scientific papers and journals, and it is likely that the institutions who publish details of their research in these journals are looking for commercial partners to help explore them.

Another member of the team could volunteer to make contact with inventors' clubs and networks. Mensa, the world-wide club for people with the highest IQs has an inventors' special interest group. Patentees can also be found at inventors' fairs and exhibitions. In the UK, the Department of Trade and Industry supports an Institute of Patentees and Inventors. In each major city in the European Union there are Business Innovation Centres (BICs). Local development agencies, new product development consultancies and venture capital organisations may also be able to facilitate useful contacts.

Searching and monitoring external sources are not only useful for extending a company's own product portfolio, it also keeps the company in touch with competitors' moves (although companies who can bear the risk might not register patents or make research public until just before product launch). It also keeps a company in touch with technology in general, which is a very important factor in a company's life expectancy.

James Utterback (1994) (Massachusetts Institute of Technology) has examined the disturbing regularity with which leading companies, throughout industrial history, have followed their core technologies into obsolescence. He traces the historical antecedents of this tendency back to the industrial revolution. In the early nineteenth century, the New England ice-cutting industry built a formidable delivery business across America. In the 1860s, ice-making machines arrived from France, but the ice-cutting industry did not embrace the new technology. The industry did not even carry the natural product south in refrigerated ships.

Utterback's research reveals that radical innovations usually come from outside the industry they most affect, and they also exist for many years before they become commercially significant. For example, early personal computers were put together in garages, and the UNIX operating system came from a unversity source.

Wide and open-minded monitoring of external sources of new product ideas is vital to a company that wants to exceed the average corporate life-span of 40 years.

Summary: external ideas – checklist of sources

- Patent Office
- National Ministry for Industry
- Local development agencies
- Scientific journals
- Academic reports
- Inventors' associations
- New product consultancies
- Venture capital organisations
- Business magazines
- Inventors' fairs

GENERATING NEEDS-BASED PRODUCT IDEAS WITHIN THE TEAM

In addition to external ideas, there are techniques for generating ideas in the team. Brainstorming, already described, is designed to stimulate quick-fire idea-skimming and will be suitable for compiling a list of potential solutions to the need in question. The team will then have to decide on the one or two solutions from the list which have most potential. Thereafter, deeper thought must be applied. The exercise recommended here is a combination of the reversal technique discussed in Chapter 1, and analogy seeking.

Reversal

I have already referred to Adrian Furnham's (*Financial Times* 6/7/ 94) application of reversal technique in relation to management theories. For example, the opposite of management by walking about (BWA) is management by hiding away. If an opposite seems absurd, the value of a proposal can be more vividly appreciated and its features developed. With product proposals, we can take the technique much further.

When it comes to using reversal technique for generating and developing new product ideas, there are two stages.

1 Reverse the need

Observed need:
- Sunbathers need portable windbreaks which provide effective shelter.

First opposite:
- Sunbathers do not need a product which gusts cold air over them.

At a superficial level, this merely states what we obviously wish to avoid in our new product deliberations. (However, a sub-committee might like to challenge the assumptions in the reversal and deduce that in some cases sunbathers might indeed like a breeze machine!)

2 Reverse the preferred solution/s from the brainstorming list

Preferred solution:
- Some form of layered, vented, lightweight sheeting might provide the best windbreak.

Second opposite:
- A material which will capture wind, rather than diffuse it.

The opposite here might be very useful for windsurfers and sailing boats, but it will not help our wind-averse sunbather. We have fixed in the minds of the new product development team what the solution is not, but how does this help innovation?

The power of the reversal technique is demonstrated when the reverses we have identified are re-reversed. You do not necessarily get the situation you started with:

First opposite:
- Sunbathers do not need a product which gusts cold air over them.

Re-reversal:
- Sunbathers need a product which blows warm air over them.

Second opposite:
- A material which will capture wind, rather than diffuse it.

Re-reversal:
- A material which has as many holes in it as possible.

These new slants on comfort whilst sunbathing could lead the development team to a product breakthrough.

Add analogy

To enhance this technique still further, analogies can be applied. What is this problem like, and how has this similar problem been solved in other environments? Even if the analogy is not very direct, reframing the problem in another setting can provide breakthrough inspiration.

In the case of the windbreak, gardeners know that the most effective windbreak in their experience is a thick conifer hedge. If there were anyone in the team with knowledge of farming, they would know that there is a form of vented fabric/plastic material used for protecting animal pens from the wind.

Nature is the richest source of analogy. Millions of years of evolution can normally be relied upon for good solutions to widespread needs. The fastening material Velcro was inspired by seed burrs. Anyone who has picked seed burrs off a jumper or out of a pet's fur knows how persistently their hooked spines cling. Paul Moller, the inventor of the flying car, was inspired by a humming bird. The bird beats its wings at tremendous speed in order to hover and reverse, which other birds cannot do. Moller set out to find a mechanical equivalent of this process.

Analogies can also be derived from team members' hobbies, domestic situations, contacts in unrelated professions and their exposure to different cultures on holiday or assignments. Wherever the analogies come from, they should be welcomed for the value they consistently add to idea-generation exercises.

EXERCISE   NEEDS-BASED SOLUTIONS – IDEA-GENERATION

What is the need?	
First opposite. What is the opposite of this need?	
Re-reversal. What is the opposite of this opposite?	
What is the likely solution to the original need?	
Second opposite. What is the opposite of this solution?	
Re-reversal. What is the opposite of this opposite?	
Potential solutions?	1
	2
What is this situation like?	1
	2
	3
Potential solutions?	1
	2
	3
	4

EVALUATION

Further chapters in the book will discuss the evaluation of product concepts in detail. However, a first pass has to be made fairly soon after an idea-generation session to reduce large quantities of ideas to a more manageable number. The following checklist may be applied as a rough guide. Score each factor out of 20 to give a total out of 100.

Template   'first pass' evaluation checklist

Question	Answer	Score
What does this idea do for the customer?	Something/nothing	
What is the maximum benefit a customer could derive?	Substantial/ negligible	
What is different about this idea?	Very different/not at all different	
What about this idea works well?	Very implementable/ difficult to implement	
What will it be like operating this idea?	Easy to use/difficult to use	
Total		

Example   'first pass' evaluation checklist

Question	Answer	Score
What does this idea do for the customer?	Something/nothing	Something – 15
What is the maximum benefit a customer could derive?	Substantial/ negligible	Not substantial, but nice to have – 8
What is different about this idea?	Very different/not at all different	Strikingly different – 18
What about this idea works well?	Very implementable/ difficult to implement	In between – 10
What will it be like operating this idea?	Easy to use/difficult to use	Difficult to use – 0
Total		*51*

SUMMARY OF CHAPTER 2

This chapter has reviewed ways of triggering new product breakthroughs.

■ Abstract generation of product ideas using forced recombinations has proved to have practical applications.
■ The opposite approach is to develop product solutions from examination of unfulfilled customer needs, which may be specific, bespoke, vague or evolving.
■ Having defined the need, solutions may be found from sources outside the company and brought in.

- Or ideas may be generated within the team by reversing and re-reversing the need and adding analogy.
- 'First pass' evaluation will then identify the concepts to progress to prototype.

3 Defining and perfecting the product core

Having generated some product ideas, convergent thinking is now required to perfect each concept. Whether your product is a tangible thing which people can see, touch and take away with them, or something more esoteric, it is important to identify the one key thing that it does for customers. A drill makes holes, a meal satisfies hunger, a paperclip holds papers together, a watch tells the time (even a very fashionable one must tell the time as well as being decorative).

The technique that can be used to identify the core function of a product is called 'murder-boarding'.

EXERCISE 'MURDER-BOARDING'

In order to live one day eternally, one must submit oneself to death many times.

(Caspar David Friedrich)

Caspar David Friedrich was a great artist who does indeed live eternally through the legacy of his spiritual landscapes. Like many artists, he periodically denigrated his own work. Similarly, product development teams need to criticise product concepts.

Murder-boarding is a negative application of brainstorming. Instead of putting forward positive ideas and suspending judgement, the team must apply judgement, and lots of it. It is an opportunity to 'murder' the product or product concept, think of everything that is wrong with it until it

> can be criticised no more. The facilitator will list all the criticisms, and at the end of the session, they can be evaluated. Some will be valid, and identify areas of improvement required in the product proposal, others will be bogus, but might provide insight into objections that sales staff will have to deal with if the product is launched.
>
> The team must then search for what is missing from the list – *what is it about the product concept which nobody can take away?* What is it that it really does for potential customers?

Identifying and understanding product 'core' can save companies money and ensure that competitive advantage is finely tuned. Many prestigious organisations learn this lesson the hard way. The US Hyatt Hotels chain suffered when the market for luxury hotels in the USA crashed in 1990. In the 1970s and 1980s, they piled on services. In the 1990s, they have had to find out what customers really want. Beds are only turned down if the customer requests it, saving $220,000 per annum in one hotel alone. Varieties of glass, silver and china have been reduced. The wine list has been cut from 380 to 38 choices. These are minor cuts which have not upset guests, they are still getting what they value in a luxury hotel, such as architectural grandeur and large, plush rooms.

In the early 1980s, the medical equipment division of German manufacturing giant Siemens was facing price competition from Japanese rivals. The pride of Germany's industry – engineering perfection – was being derided as 'over-engineering' by customers no longer willing to pay for it. Siemens had to embark on a radical cost-cutting programme, which the company's engineers found hard to take. They are trained to design the best, not to design to target cost. Siemens wanted cost cuts of 40 per cent. It was deemed laughable, impossible, but in the end they achieved 50 per cent cost reduction. This was done for the most part by cutting the number of features and controls. These efforts ensured that Siemens maintained market share, and they were able to increase R&D spend on new products.

DIMENSIONS OF 'CORE' QUALITY – PHYSICAL PRODUCTS

The murder-boarding session should have identified the core benefit offered by the product concept. Now the team needs to discuss how well that core benefit is delivered. The principles recommended for this evaluation are Professor David Garvin's (quoted in Schonberger and Knod, 1991) eight dimensions of quality:

- Conformance
- Aesthetics
- Reliability
- Serviceability
- Durability
- Performance
- Features
- Perceived quality

Professor Garvin is the chief advocate of a broad view of quality. He also believes that the definition of quality should shift as products move through design and development towards delivery. So the product concept must be regularly measured against his standards. Indeed, even after a product has been launched, and throughout its growth phase, there is always potential for quality review and improvement. The product development team might even take a product in its mature stage, murder-board it and rebuild it for a new lease of life.

Conformance

The first thing that a product or service must do to justify its existence is to conform to what is expected of it, but what does that mean? Conformance was defined by Garvin (1991) as 'meeting specifications', but what is also required is conformance to the customer's need. No product can succeed if it does not do what the customer wants. A drill which does not make holes will not be bought. Statutes have been passed in the USA and Europe to ensure that companies actually supply goods and services which not only do what they say, but do what they imply. Consumers also have the right under contract law to bring civil cases against sellers who make false claims.

If a product concept survives a murder-boarding session with the planning team confident that it meets the customer need it is intended to address, the outlook is promising.

However, it is also important to look at customer usage. The concept must work in a way which supports likely usage patterns, or it may founder in its growth phase. For example, early bank automated teller machines gave out money before the customer's card was returned, consequently, many people forgot to collect their cards. Apart from costing a lot of money to fix, that usage problem could have deterred users and potential users.

Rubbermaid of the USA is well known for understanding the way their customers use their products, and they make it easier for them. Because most women carry laundry baskets on their hip, Rubbermaid shaped their laundry basket to make that easier.

It is possible these days, with the benefit of computer-aided design, virtual reality and rapid prototyping technology, to bring new products to test very quickly. Everything from aero engines to Easter egg packaging could be tested for ease of use quite early in its development.

Twenty years of research at the Univeristy of Pennsylvania have produced a virtual human who is used to test the design of vehicles and other large machines operated by humans. Vickers has used 'Jack' software to assess engine designs for ease of maintenance and John Deere has used it to test everything from bulldozers to garden equipment. 'Jack' has a feature which allows the design engineer to see through its virtual eyes, so problems of visual interference can be solved in advance of prototyping.

After virtual usage testing, the product can proceed to rapid prototyping. Rapid prototyping bureaux can convert CAD (computer-aided design) files into resin prototypes within a few hours for a small component and a few days for a large item. The process cuts out months of model-making. One RP bureau in the UK has prototyped everything from a mobile phone to a human skull for clinical studies.

Usage is not just a matter of convenience, there are also safety considerations. When consumers find that a lead on a power tool is too short or a pan handle is awkward, using the product results in irritation and possible danger as they try their own adaptations. For years UK consumers put up with buying electrical goods without plugs attached – goods technically unfit for use. They had to fit their own but, of course, they were not trained plug fitters. Thousands of domestic accidents were caused by badly fitted plugs, and the Consumers' Association forced the UK government to legislate to require manufacturers to fit integral plugs.

Think of medical machines – if they do not conform to user requirements, people die. The IDEO company in the USA designed an infusion pump (for McGaw) for delivering drugs to a patient intravenously. They found, by involving nurses in testing the equipment, that doses were best programmed using a volume control rather than a keypad – it eliminated the risks of large errors in dosage due to 'finger trouble'.

Conformance is not just a matter of meeting analysts' specifications or industry standards, although these things may also contribute to the success of a product. The critical conformance criteria are to meet customer need and to facilitate hassle-free access to that need.

EXERCISE   ROLE-PLAY

In order to practise taking a broad view of conformance criteria, members of the team may try the following role-plays. What would they need, as users, to really get the most out of these products?

- If I were using a can opener
- If I were an office cleaner using a vacuum cleaner
- If I were Richard Nixon using a tape recorder
- If I were Elizabeth Taylor repairing an aeroplane engine
- If I were a hairdresser using an electronic shopping terminal
- If I were a lorry driver using a mobile phone

Aesthetics

Although not second in Professor Garvin's original list, it is worthy of note that in many countries, a design can be protected for longer than an invention. So it is critical to the competitive advantage of the product to consider the physical attractiveness attributes of a product at an early stage.

The Japanese define aesthetics as attributes which make a product desirable. An aesthetic product has a favourable impact on the senses of the customer – their ears, eyes, touch (and taste and smell in some cases). Even the most utilitarian of products can be made more desirable by applying colour and style. Slough Borough Council recently painted the town's main car park a pastel pink on the advice of psychologists. It was part of a package of measures to deal with fear of crime in car parks. Even those who initially thought that it was a joke had to admit that it was an improvement on the bare dingy grey of most multi-storey car parks.

Companies use art and graphic design students to marry technology with design. A US computer firm commissioned students at London's Royal College of Art to produce fashion designs for technological products. One of the successes of this commission is a mobile-telephone glove.

Aesthetics is not just about colour and style. Sometimes, customers have a physical need for aesthetic improvements. Excess noise can damage people's health. Active noise cancellation (ANC) technology has been around for 60 years and is finally moving out of the laboratory and into the market-place. An ANC system detects a sound and cancels it out by generating a second sound wave. It is now available on Saab commercial aircraft, reducing noise in the cabin. It can be used in heating and air-conditioning systems. Consumer goods are very price-sensitive, but Electrolux are introducing it into cooker hoods. Nissan have tried it in cars.

Anything which people have to touch or feel has to be particularly carefully researched. In the 1960s, nylon was used in clothes and bedding, but hated because water vapour could not pass through it and it made people feel uncomfortable. Manufacturers have since developed ultra-fine filaments of nylon which, when woven together in a garment, produce pores which allow water vapour out, but are small enough to prevent water or wind getting in. So, in the 1990s, nylon is back in fashionable sportswear. However, the inventors of nylon, Du Pont, and other nylon manufacturers, have shrewdly chosen some new brand names for it.

Aesthetics can deliver competitive advantage, and the more integral it is to a product, the more difficult it might be to imitate.

EXERCISE   GROUP DISCUSSION

Our tastes are as individual as we are – or are they?
Each member of the team must bravely discuss the colours, shapes, sounds and textures that they like (and perhaps even smells and tastes). If any preferences are mentioned more than three times, discuss how they might be applied to the product concept. Would the result of any of these applications constitute a personality for the product?

Reliability

The zero-defects concept was developed by Philip Crosby – and indeed, what is the alternative? It costs money to put things right, and in times of immense pressure on costs, the pursuit of zero defects is just plain common sense. Customers expect it too!

We take quality products for granted now partly because the Japanese used quality as their competitive advantage in entering American and European markets. New technology has also made it easier to deliver reliable products. Quality has also been driven by consumer pressure groups in the USA and Europe, demanding better standards. In fact, in the USA in the 1980s there was a product liability insurance crisis because consumers were suing manufacturers over unreliable products so frequently.

In the 1960s, consumers bought their white and brown goods primarily from home suppliers. Televisions used to break down, cars used to break down. Throughout the 1970s and 1980s, consumers in the USA and Europe started to transfer their preference to brands perceived to be reliable. They were predominantly Japanese. Japanese manufacturers were learning from American exponents of quality and the rest of the world was not. W. Edwards Deming was a hero in Japan 30 years before he was recognised in his native USA. Japan's top quality prize is named after him.

Deming (quoted in Schonberger and Knod, 1991) is famous for his fourteen points, which concentrate on achieving the reliability of products through the elimination of defects.

Summary of Deming's 14 points

- **Constancy of purpose towards improvement of product/service** – Deming believed that there was never any room for complacency in the pursuit of quality.
- **Adopt the new philosophy, 'we cannot live with defects'** – apart from the logic of his arguments, Deming also saw quality as an evangelical crusade, as much about hearts as minds.
- **Prevent rather than detect defects** – at the time Deming was writing, quality assurance in the USA and Europe was a matter of policing. Deming knew that prevention was better and cheaper than cure.
- **Don't choose suppliers on price, choose on quality** – many supplier–customer negotiations in business-to-business markets are adversarial and concentrate on price, even though many other things matter in the relationship. A number of world-class manufacturers have extended Deming's beliefs about buying on quality and made suppliers virtually 'partners' in their enterprise through single sourcing.
- **Find problems** – most people are internally motivated to hide problems, but if quality matters, problems must be out in the open where they can be dealt with.
- **Train people** – everybody must be prepared for the job they are asked to do. Deming had no time for the 'sink-or-swim' approach.
- **Managers must act upon the concerns of production supervisors** – it is important to listen to people close to the production process. Buck-passing, attempts to suppress issues and asking workers to 'make do' must be eliminated if quality is to be achieved.

■ **Drive out fear** – workers who live in fear of the boss or the sack are under negative stress and therefore not at their productive best.

■ **Break down barriers between departments** – the need for cross-departmental co-operation has already been discussed.

■ **Don't exhort your people to greater productivity without giving them the methods to deliver it** – operators are probably already doing their best within the system and resources that they have at their disposal. If more is required, it is the job of management to seek better processes and methods and introduce them.

■ **Eliminate numerical quotas** – this is quite difficult to imagine, but with technology enabling a just-in-time approach to manufacturing, it is perfectly acceptable for production to fluctuate with demand.

■ **Remove barriers between the worker and his craft** – everybody has a right to take pride in their work. If workers are isolated from the fruit of their labour, and from other people who contribute to the product, alienation is the result. Many of the strikes in the 1960s, when factory workers did single monotonous tasks now usually performed by robots, were attributed to boredom. Teamwork approaches to production enable workers to identify with each other and with a job well done.

■ **Educate and retrain** – the pace of change in technology and commerce means that education and retraining are now for life.

■ **Create a system to ensure top management push all this**! Top management have to take their eye off the bottom line in the short term in order to protect it in the long term. World class companies in the 1990s do take quality very seriously and make it as much a part of regular reporting requirements as revenue and profit.

The weight of evidence that defect-free output delivers reduced cost of operations and is critical in order to compete speaks for itself. Nevertheless, in some parts of the world, and in some sectors of the developed economies, quality is still not all it could be; Deming's quest goes on.

EXERCISE SCENARIO-BUILDING 1

> Imagine a a day when everything goes wrong:
> You wake up in a waterbed which is leaking. The toaster does not toast your bread, it makes it rubbery. The knife you use to butter your bread is floppy – it can't even cut the butter, which is rancid anyway. The clothes you put on do not keep you warm or preserve your modesty. You try to clean your teeth, but instead of making them whiter, the toothpaste makes them black.
> Each of the team can add an episode to this story. The moral is that products that customers cannot rely on are very depressing. Even simple things need to be defect-free in order to be merely satisfactory, let alone delightful.

Serviceability

The less parts or processes there are to go wrong, the more serviceable a product is. Simplicity has to accommodate the future as well as the present. Manufacturers could even anticipate technological advance so that products could be upgraded with more powerful motors, for example. Products should be made in a modular way – easy to disassemble and reassemble. The likelihood of customers mixing and matching a product with other manufacturer's parts also has to be accommodated. It can be claimed as an advantage.

Serviceability alone can change an industry. Integration and upgradeability are very important in computer systems. In the 1980s, demand for 'open' systems moved from academic circles to commerce and swept new manufacturers like Sun Microsystems into the big league.

Schonberger and Knod (1991) developed guidelines for serviceability in *Operations Management.* The overriding principle they recommend is to design to target cost, not estimated cost. Target cost, naturally, should be in line with target sales and target profit. This challenge can enhance the creativity of the product development team, as it requires them to explore various ways of doing things.

Minimising part counts and numbers of operations is critical to achieving lower cost, better quality, better production and better service. Similarly, using standard materials, parts and procedures is important. Rank Xerox was failing in the early 1980s, partly because of the unique nature of its machines – every nut in every model of photocopier was different, a special. Design complexity led to extensive field-service requirements for sold copiers. The cost of spares was high and the cost of specialist labour to do repairs was high. Now Xerox uses standard parts.

New products or services should work within tolerances that will not strain people or machines. If processes of manufacture and use are to be successful, they must not expect the highest performance from machines or people.

Products should be also easy to hold and less heavy than what has gone before – even if the team is developing an aero engine, making it weigh less can be a valuable technological advance. Once again, the example of Japanese companies and their success in making things smaller and lighter is worth emulating.

Shapes should be easy for packing and unpacking. Odd protrusions can lead to product or user damage. Configure parts to avoid difficult angles and tight squeezes. It is also worth ensuring that components fasten together simply. Parts that can be pushed into place (like PC boards on a rack) will be more serviceable that parts that have to be screwed together.

Serviceability is an aspect of product design which can deliver competitive advantage in terms of potential to improve profitability and convenience to the customer.

EXERCISE ABSTRACTIONS

Imagine ways in which the following could be made more serviceable:

■ A dog
■ A shoe
■ A restaurant
■ A car engine
■ A telephone
■ A political system
■ A road

Durability

The requirement for a product to be durable is covered by legislation in some countries, e.g. in the UK by the Sale of Goods Act. Consumer associations are calling for the mandatory labelling of the expected life-span of products and pressurising manufacturers for longer guarantees. Life-spans do vary, and once again we find an aspect of quality which, if explored, might deliver competitive advantage, but, if ignored, would mark out a product as an also-ran.

The average life-span of a washing machine manufactured in the UK is 7-10 years. In Finland, ASKO produce models which will last 15; Swedish manufacturers ensure 17. Washing machines can be made more durable by electronic controls without moving parts, by using the hardest enamels which do not yellow and high-grade stainless steel for the drum. German manufacturers have concentrated on ensuring that the drum suspension can cope with a great deal of stress.

If serviceability has been ensured, there should be no incentive for any manufacturer to dream about building obsolescence into a product. Customers will want to buy upgrades and add-ons. Their brand loyalty will be assured for longer. A manufacturer might also be able to exploit the second-hand market. Black and Decker have special outlets selling reconditioned power tools, having recognised that there are some items householders would usually hire that they might buy on a special deal.

Ensuring extended regular use of products is an opportunity for companies to excel. And, whilst manufacturers usually cringe about having to anticipate customer misuse, going that bit further is an additional aspect of differentiation of a product in its core function. Things get dropped. Children load their sandwiches into video machines and wedge sugared oats between the keys on computer keyboards. Products get left in the heat or the cold or the wet.

If products are launched without due attention to durability, the diffusion of innovation curve may crack back at the manufacturer with a vengeance. Early adopters who have to send their purchases to the repair shop are likely to tell nine early majority buyers not to bother. On the other hand, the manufacturer who anticipates a long lifetime of use, and also saves the customer from their own potential misuse, deserves to be preferred.

EXERCISE   SCENARIO-BUILDING 2

Let's revisit the dreadful day when nothing worked. This time, the things work, but show instant signs of wear:
The bed frame is scuffed, the toaster is yellow, the knife handle is stained, the toothbrush bristles are splayed.
The team can introduce new episodes illustrating aspects of use, and perhaps misuse, which disappoint customers.

Performance

Schonberger and Knod (1991) interpret Garvin's quality factor of performance as the product's capacity to exceed expectations and be award-winning. Once a product is award-winning, it acquires intangible features of excellence. It is natural for a product team to want to deliver a best-in-class item, such as mobile phone of the year or personal computer of the month or an entry in a prestigious restaurant guide. However, there are any number of other awards which could set a product apart from its peers – such as design awards and service awards.

EXERCISE   SCENARIO-BUILDING 3

Imagine an Oscar ceremony for your product type:

■ What are the judges looking for?
■ What do the gushing nominees and acceptors say?

Features

As discussed earlier, many customers are not interested in paying for special features. Think of all the features that are built in to software packages and hi-fi systems which the majority of users never touch. Microsoft scored with Works because, whilst their country managers fretted about function, customers just wanted the basics to get going with desk-top computing, and that was what Works was all about.

EXERCISE   'SO WHAT?' + REVERSAL

In order to test the value of each proposed feature in a product or service, the 'so what?' technique should be applied. If this fails to reduce the list of desirables, try adding the reversal technique.

For example:

Our car radio must have two more pre-programmable channels than the previous model.

So what if our car radio had two *less* than the previous model? How many favourite radio stations do customers actually have?

Less channels with better reception might be the more appropriate answer to the customer needs.

Some features could even wait until a product has established itself. If product failure rates are high, and even with the most careful approach, the risks are still high, why bother with features until there is some feedback about what customers would value? Discerning 1990s' customers are unlikely to be impressed by features alone, but features will be required in due course to cater to the great god of choice. If serviceability has been built in, the extras market could be very profitable.

Alternatively, with some types of product or service, a large number of modules could be made available for customers to pick and mix. IBM's Catia (CAD/CAM software) has 48 modules – customers don't have to buy the whole thing, only what they need. Few companies need every feature of a CAD/CAM system, and fewer still can afford them. They must buy only what fits their business strategy – providing improved efficiency, quality and time to market. Product variation will be discussed at greater length in a later chapter.

Perceived quality

Garvin said this means the product has a mystique about it, and Schonberger and Knod (1991) added to his interpretation of perceived quality. They defined perceived quality as incorporating the customer's sense of value for money. Other aspects of the 'mystique' include the responsiveness of the company in delivering new products to meet needs (time-based manufacturing) and their humanity in dealing with customer needs. Schonberger and Knod interpret humanity as company-wide courtesy and understanding towards customers. They also define the mystique of perceived quality as a sense of security, a feeling that this manufacturer's products will be safe, and a confidence in the competency of the firm. Customers can trust that the firm employs people with the skills and knowledge appropriate to producing, supplying and servicing this product.

DIMENSIONS OF CORE QUALITY FOR SERVICE PRODUCTS

The formula I have chosen for core quality in service products comes from Leonard Berry and colleagues at Texas A&M University, who spent most of the 1980s studying service quality in the

USA. They emphasise that customers are the sole arbiters of service quality. When managers take it upon themselves to decide what the customers want, bizarre anomalies occur. They give the example of a large hotel which had been established for 15 years before it was realised that two-thirds of all guest calls to housekeeping were to request an iron and ironing board. The hotel had budgeted to upgrade bathroom televisions from black and white to colour, something no guest had ever requested. They decided to switch that budget to providing irons and ironing boards in every room. Apart from giving the customers what they actually wanted, it improved the productivity of the housekeeping department.

The dimensions of service quality which Berry et al. found to be important to customers of service industries were:

- Reliability
- Tangibles
- Responsiveness
- Assurance
- Empathy

Reliability

People hate to be let down. The classic culprits are mini-cab firms whose interpretation of customers' booking times are usually at least liberal and sometimes callous. Berry et al. say that keeping the service promise is the absolute 'core' that the customer expects. In all their research, this was rated the single most important thing. If a company is not dependable, they are not used again. Years ago, when people took time off work to wait in for a repair to be done, companies gave no indication when in the day the engineer might turn up. Most companies now give approximate appointment times and keep in touch with their repair staff by mobile phone and data links so that any timekeeping problems can be quickly addressed.

Reliability has to be total. Who wants to be operated on by a surgeon who is 'usually reliable'? Who wants to travel on a ship whose navigation officer is 'usually reliable', or entrust money to a financial institution which is 'usually reliable'? Even 99 per cent reliability is suspect. As Berry et al. point out, that would mean nine misspelt words on every page of a magazine, and unsafe drinking water four times a year. It is constant hard work to always keep the service promise, but the rewards are high in terms of winning and keeping customers. Trust is a very powerful bond between people and organisations. It is a critical ingredient in partnership sourcing.

EXERCISE   'MURDER-BOARDING'

> If reliability is what matters most to customers, work out what your core service promise is.
> Brainstorm all the criticisms of your service and subsequently deduce what it is that cannot be taken away, the core thing which you are doing for the customer.

Tangibles

The physical attributes of facilities, equipment and personnel do matter to the customers of service industries. This dimension can be related to Garvin's aesthetics. In service delivery, the list of attributes will include things like clean floors and smart uniforms as well as good design in the reception area.

Customers are rarely explicit about the 'tangibles' of service quality, they may have to be deduced from other descriptions. A UK library service recently researched the dimensions of their service which were most important to their customers. They were ranked as follows:

- Library staff
- Book and journal collection (range)
- Reliability of computer system
- Environmental factors (temperature, light)
- Library rules
- Speed of access to photocopiers
- Library information
- Availability of stock
- Noise levels

Environmental factors would clearly come under the heading of tangibles, but there is an element of tangibility about the appearance of staff, range of books and library information.

EXERCISE BRAINSTORM

What physical attributes are included in your service delivery?

Responsiveness

The willingness of staff to help, and promptly, is important to customers, but is all too often a rare experience for them. This aspect of service will be discussed again in the next chapter.

Assurance

Customers are reassured by service deliverers who are knowledgeable and confident. They also expect them to be polite. Courtesy is very highly rated in Japan as an aspect of service. It is becoming more important in Europe and the USA.

Empathy

Service companies who value their customers must listen to them. It is one thing to be in a market segment of millions for a widget or a can of beans, but for service we would all like to be in a market segment of one! So many service companies are small businesses because they can provide the individual care that customers enjoy.

DIMENSIONS OF CORE QUALITY FOR INTANGIBLE PRODUCTS

Intangibles relating to products are discussed in detail in the next chapter, but it would be wrong to leave a chapter about product 'cores' without mentioning that some products are completely lacking in physical attributes, but still have a core to be defined and refined. The person who visits a manicurist comes away from the experience with good-looking nails as well as (hopefully) a good feeling. An intangible product can only get at your spirit, it does nothing physical at all.

The company has always been about exploring, taking risks and developing new ways of working. We use movement to intensify and heighten emotion, and by moving the actor physically, hope to move the audience emotionally.

(extract from mission statement, Shared Experience Theatre Company)

I was still so wound up in the play when I got home that I got into the bath with my clothes on!
We were all quite exhausted at the end of the show!
I came away buzzing!

(audience reaction)

Fecundly inventive.
not only reinvents the book, but pushes the boat of theatricality way beyond its usual moorings.

(critics' reaction)

Everyday, there are professional people taking on the challenge of delivering 'products' to people which consist only of emotional benefits. The product *is* what the customer *feels* about it. It is even more abstract than a service. In using the example of artistic performance, I am separating the product of the performing company from the service provided by the theatre in which it is staged, which does have physical attributes.

How can intangibles' 'cores' be developed?

Shared Experience has a strong artistic policy which governs the style and content of productions and builds on their powerful reputation for turning difficult-to-read novels into exciting plays. The mix of tours, workshops and masterclasses is important, and the need 'to be even more productive, exciting, boundary-breaking, innovative, inspiring' is well recognised. The impact of the plays has to be rigorously rehearsed, the script and cast well-chosen.

Strategy can also be applied to develop the cultural and educational intangibles provided by a library, or the intangibles of youth clubs, which affect parents and society as well as the young people who attend them.

Tom Peters (1989) has come up with some dimensions of quality which he originally applied to an 'experience' restaurant, but which suit intangible products in general.

- Wow!
- Surprise!
- Holy Toledo!
- Subversive
- Heart
- Lively
- Beyond satisfaction
- I'll know it when I see it

Good entertainment usually provides all of these, but it can be a challenge for developers of less glamorous products to know how to apply them. Nevertheless, even charities rasing money for the most tragic of causes have to shock and subvert their prospects, appeal to their hearts and convince them that they will be more than satisfied to make a donation.

SUMMARY OF CHAPTER 3

There may be alternatives to ensuring integral quality in a product's core function, but the only main benefit that might accrue from the alternatives is the lessons everybody in the company learns about such diversions. Of course, very innovative companies cannot be 100 per cent sure that the function of their product will hit the customer's need spot-on. One hugely successful international scientific company explained to me that they never bid for new requirements which they thought they could not meet, but nevertheless, since they are at the forefront of technology, they still have to take risks with what they think they can do. The important thing is to do a lot of thinking and testing as early in

Figure 4.1 Onion diagram

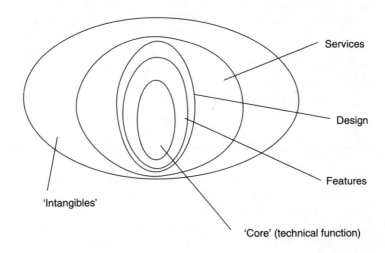

when their name is on the machine, and someone has paid $2,000 for it, they expect good service. Manufacturers of personal computers may say that it is a commodity market, but to each user, it is a major purchase.

DEFINING MEASURABLE SERVICE

One of the Latin words for service, 'opera', is also translated as 'trouble, pains, exertion'.

Organisations naturally fear that providing services and developing intangibles will be costly, but it is effective service that matters; this can be relatively inexpensive and can deliver differentiation and competitive advantage.

■ BOC Gases defended its 60 per cent market share of the UK industrial gas market from European Union competitors with a service initiative. The company introduced a freephone single point of contact for customer enquiries. Each operator is trained to answer queries on everything from cylinder transport storage to

the use of inert gases in confined spaces, as well as handling orders and complaints.
- Dental supplies company Schein Rexodent grew from zero to £30 million turnover in the UK in 10 years. The founders of the company say that they were able to enter and grow in a very tight market because their competitors made the mistake of thinking that they were only about low prices. In fact, Rexodent used service to win customers. Fulfilment rates are 98 per cent, and they guarantee same-day dispatch for orders received up to 6 p.m.

Service is often inextricably intertwined with intangibles, but there is a difference which the new product development team can easily manage. In terms of the product concept, we can isolate services from intangibles as those factors which can be measured by objective criteria. For example; the following list is drawn from reports of the 1994 'Customer Champion Awards' sponsored by the *Sunday Times* and Unisys. It covers the *measurable* aspects of service which appear to matter to the customers who nominated the award winners and thus are delivering competitive advantage:

Service guarantees should be bold, clear and relevant, for example:

- Time guarantees (e.g. your pizza will be delivered within 30 minutes, your lathe will be repaired between 8 a.m. and 11 a.m. tomorrow) – excellent companies usually average much less than the time they guarantee
- Limits on time in queues, e.g. 90 per cent of customers to wait no longer than five minutes
- Customer enquiries and letters should be answered within a (short) guaranteed time
- Being open/accessible when customers can use the service – for example, a jeweller opening at 8 a.m. to enable customers to deposit or collect repairs on the way to work
- High order-fulfilment rates (95 per cent+)
- Total accuracy in paperwork (put in place targets to reduce paperwork!)
- Automatic compensation if a guarantee is not met

Organisations can also measure themselves on other service attributes which the customer values such as:

■ A single, human point of contact
■ Seeking regular feedback from customers, e.g. postal questionnaires about service
■ Free, relevant accessories – such as the right polish with a piece of furniture
■ Knowledgeable staff – one UK Do-It-Yourself chain received a lot of favourable press for preferring to recruit mature people with experience of DIY to teenagers; they had realised that prospective customers needed to talk to sales staff who understood what they were trying to achieve in their homes and gardens and could suggest the appropriate equipment.

DEFINING INTANGIBLES

Beyond good service, and sometimes before customers get to try the service, there is something more that they value.

We want to influence the feeling the customer has in the pit of his stomach when he deals with our company.
(Nigel Russell, Marketing and Customer Service Manager, Securicor Cellular Services)

Quality doesn't have to be defined. Quality is a direct experience independent of and prior to intellectual abstractions.
(Robert Pirsig)

Intangibles cannot easily be measured and are subjective by their nature: 'It enhances my day to be served by pleasant, courteous, caring and knowledgeable staff.' Nevertheless, companies and public services are appreciating the value of doing things which help customers to feel good about them.Companies that endeavour to be ethical, keep in touch with social trends, e.g. interest in the environment, and treat customers, suppliers and employees well can see benefits from those policies in their bottom line. Getting involved in sponsorship and community activities also can be more effective than traditional advertising. DEC used arts sponsorship as a promotional route into the UK computer market in the 1970s.

In order to define which intangibles matter to customers, there is no better way than to experience what it is like to be a customer.

WHICH INTANGIBLES MATTER?

The customer, of course, does not have to define and disentangle services and intangibles. All they have to consider is how they feel about a company or product, based on personal experience. Whatever the Chief Executive of an organisation thinks about its products or services, whatever the advertising slogans say, customers will make their own judgement based on what happens to them in connection with that product or service.

Researching the customer experience to assess whether it is 'feelgood' or 'feelbad' is extremely easy. An approach said to be at the heart of the genius of physicist Richard Feynman was his ability to ask himself, 'If I were an electron, what would I do?' I would suggest that it is the mark of business genius to ask: 'If I were a customer, what would I *feel*?'

John Spiers, Chairman of the Brighton Health Care Trust, took to a wheelchair to test the service he is in charge of providing. A project manager at a Cranfield client volunteered to spend two weeks working for a customer to feel what it was like dealing with his company. Key accounts often exchange staff in order to improve relationships and processes. Organisations with large numbers of geographically dispersed customers, such as the Automobile Association, electrical retailers Comet and McDonalds, commission specialist market researchers called 'mystery shoppers'. In addition to playing 'the real customer', planning teams can also enhance experience-based research by exploring 'what-if' scenarios.

One of the great maxims of marketing is that if customers have a good experience with a product or service, they will tell three people. If they have a bad experience they will tell at least nine. Company decision-makers may be less likely to exchange notes about bad purchases, but the end users' grapevine will compensate for that reticence. The anecdotes vary. Virgin believes that where flights are concerned, people recount a good experience four times and a bad one 17 times. What has also been noted by the *Financial Times* in a review of airline service is the length of time that customers bear grudges for bad flights. One business traveller wrote into the newspaper about bad service he had received from an airline company in 1953!

Allied Breweries estimate that a customer who has a bad pint in a pub tells 13 people, and if they all go and drink somewhere else for a year it costs the brewery £11,000. You would not have to listen long to any conversation in a canteen or a corridor to realise the truth of this marketing maxim. We moan about a bad buy to gain sympathy, to warn others and to exact some degree of revenge on the perpetrators of our discomfort.

Customer care consultants always warn clients that customers who have bad experiences tell everyone *but* the supplier, the person who might be able to do something about it!

The other side of this scenario is the opportunity represented by positive 'word of mouth' from satisfied customers. Tom Peters devoted a whole chapter to it in *Thriving on Chaos*, even advocating that 75 per cent of marketing effort (dollars and energy) should be devoted to activating a word-of-mouth network. Reference selling is much favoured by sales representatives.

LIVING THE CUSTOMER EXPERIENCE

John Spiers, a successful businessman who took the job of Chair of a health service trust, went through fear, extreme cold and indignity when he set out to discover 'the invisible hospital – the one patients experience but which the managers never see' (as quoted in the tabloid *Daily Mirror*). He was left in the cold for 40 minutes because the hospital door was not wide enough for wheelchair access. He received extreme verbal abuse from a porter and he was left in a freezing cubicle looking at dirty fingerprints on a leaking ceiling for five hours, dressed in an embarrassingly incomplete hospital gown. He was made to feel a fool because he did not know his 'K' number. All of these experiences contravened the Trust's policy of 'positive customer care'. He commented in the *Mirror* article: 'The whole experience made me feel I had no power, no choice.'

Mr Spiers' experiment attracted extensive publicity. How many people would put themselves through so much in order to develop true empathy with customers? Yet it is obvious that to see vividly how your organisation could improve, you must feel what the customers feel. Companies that win awards are predictable in their managers' espousal of the level of service they would wish to be applied to themselves as customers. Some even practise it. Ducal Furniture requires staff periodically to unbox and assemble a piece of furniture, to remind them what customers have to do.

Organisations must explore the 'intangibles', those things which cannot be easily measured, but make a great difference to the customer feeling of being cared for. In order to do so, the product development team can start the process by engaging in role-play. Fortunately, in most cases, they would not have to be as brave as Mr Spiers. There are a number of simple spot-checks which would establish a basic understanding of what it feels like to be your own customer. The following exercise incorporates both measurable aspects of service and subjective intangibles. Team members will start to note how they are linked. For example, BT advises its business subscribers that if they do not answer the telephone within three rings, they start to denigrate the caller's self-esteem. The assumption is made, if they are keeping me waiting they cannot want my business that much.

EXERCISE   MAKING A PRODUCT ENQUIRY BY TELEPHONE

A recent survey in the UK revealed that consumers trying to obtain information by telephone from retailers were not being treated very professionally: 20 per cent of retailers took longer than five rings to answer; 20 per cent of calls had to be transferred, which took on average longer than 30 seconds and meant that consumers had to repeat their enquiries; then they were kept waiting an average of 48 seconds (although one-third waited over three minutes), for the information to be found. Whilst staff were reported to be friendly, they were obviously not well-equipped to facilitate a sale.

Each member of the product development team is to call the company with a product enquiry, and make notes on the following:

- How many rings before the switchboard answers?
- Is the operator welcoming or brusque?
- Do you get put on hold?
- How long for?
- Does the person who answers take responsibility for solving your enquiry?
- Have you been put through to the right place?
- If you are not, and have to be transferred, how long does it take?
- How long does it take to get the information that you want?
- Does everybody give his/her name clearly, and welcome you?
- Are they just taking notes, or taking an interest in your needs?
- Do you get sufficient information about when, where and how you could purchase the product?
- Are you thanked for your enquiry?
- Are you encouraged to ring again if you have any further queries?

Having replaced the receiver, ask yourself:
- Was I impressed by a friendly and efficient approach?
- Was I irritated by a just about adequate approach?
- Was I dismayed by total disinterest?

Then use the example below to complete the template.

Example   telephone response (Value = score out of 10)

Service factor	*Score*	*Value*	Intangible	*Value*
Number of rings to answer	5 rings	7	They are quite prompt	6
			Operator is cheerful – likes to talk to customers	9
Time on hold	0	10	Somebody is waiting to deal with me	10
			Someone takes responsibility for my query	10
Name given?	No	0		
			This person sounds a little aloof	4
Time to answer query	50 seconds	7		
Sufficient information	Yes	8		
Thanks given?	No	0		
			I was dealt with effectively	5
Totals		32		44
Maximum score		60		60

Template   telephone response results

Service factor	Score	Value	Intangible	Value

Although all managers should try to put themselves in their customers' shoes from time to time, it would also be good practice to seek more broadly based feedback.

Delegating customer role-play – mystery shoppers

Mystery shopping is a market research technique which involves specially trained fieldworkers visiting sales or service outlets, acting as customers and assessing the outlet and the staff on a number of points chosen by the client. This specialised market research was initially developed as a response to concern about lack of service in shops. In 1992, journalist Lynne Truss parodied the rudeness of shop assistants in *The Times*. She said: 'My latest idea is to carry a little Sooty glove puppet, so that I can produce it at key moments and talk to it when nobody else is volunteering.' Many retailers could learn from grocer Stew Leonard in Tom Peters' *Thriving on Chaos* (1989) who chooses outgoing, friendly people for his stores because 'We can teach cash register. We can't teach nice.' Mystery shopping is now used in a variety of organisations to check the service and other intangible aspects of their customer interfaces.

In the *Financial Times*, Ansells claimed that its 600 managed pubs had increased their market share in two years since the company had started to use 'mystery shoppers' to monitor them. In the Ansells case, the researchers highlighted the importance of clean toilets and friendly bar staff. If you have 600 outlets and you want to improve them all, this type of continuous monitoring by professional, analytical customers can be very helpful.

The Victoria Wine mystery shopper checklist has 51 different elements that need to be appraised within a few seconds of entering the shop, such as cleanliness and customer acknowledgement. As a result, the company has become sensitive to the matters of detail that really impress customers. They have incorporated them into training programmes, winning the British government's national training award.

The important thing for companies to remember about using mystery shoppers is that they are *professional* shoppers. In 1995, a tabloid newspaper commissioned mystery shoppers to investigate and report back on service in Britain's major retailers. Their story was headlined 'Service with a snarl'. The stores concerned were later contacted by the newspaper and most commented that they conducted their own customer research and did not get such bad ratings. Of course not. When customers are asked whether or not they are satisfied with a service, if they have never experienced best practice their feedback is likely to be optimistic. If standards are generally bad, customers can only indicate to a supplier that they are more or less bad than their peers. The same is true for business-to-business markets. Many suppliers measure their customer satisfaction from questionnaires completed by purchasing decision-makers over a coffee with their main contacts, the account managers. Such research can hardly be considered objective. Obviously, suppliers must consult customers and prospective customers to ensure that their needs are met. But if they want to *perform* rather than *norm*, they must test themselves against aspirational standards and use professional service-assessors as well.

Team members role-playing customers in fictional scenarios

Even if a new product development team is fortunate enough to have the resources to commission market research, the team can also use workshop techniques to work out how to develop product intangibles in order to enhance the customer experience.

Such an exercise should start with a provocative scenario, for example, what would you do if it were legal for customers to emit a spray with a noxious dye every time they encounter a 'feelbad' factor? This is an extreme example. However, the element of dangerous mischief can help concentration. Stirring controversy and emotion can help our thinking too. Most of us have been in situations where we wished we could have taken such direct action. So, the first stage of a creative discussion about customer experience is to consider what has provoked us in the past week. If the noxious dye reaction were legal, when would we have used it?

What is the trigger point? How long would you wait in a queue behind someone with intricately complex financial affairs, longing for a new till to open, before dousing the building society's logo on the carpet? How many abandoned shelf-fillers' pallets would you gingerly negotiate with your shopping trolley before turning one of them putrid purple? The team may need some time to think through scenarios, they may even prefer to draw them rather than talk about them. However, after about 30 minutes on a scenario, it is time to move on.

Having worked out what irks us, we can turn that behaviour on its head and work out what would please us. What if it became custom and practice to reward 'feelgood factors' everywhere with a 15 per cent gratuity? If every invoice or till receipt were left open to contributions, like credit card slips in restaurants, what would inspire payment? Effectively, when companies believe that their products command a price premium, they are suggesting a product intangible which has a value that the customer volunteers to pay. This sort of assumption just has to be tested.

Team members role-playing superachievers as customers

An enjoyable additional exercise is to role-play superachievers as customers. Start by thinking about what comic hero Superman would be like as a customer. Then imagine team members' favourite superachievers buying your products or services. How would Mother Theresa behave as a customer? Garibaldi? Einstein? Bismarck? Marie Curie? Akio Morita? Winston Churchill? Beethoven? Nelson Mandela? Leonardo da Vinci? Napoleon?

The team members should draw a cartoon of their role-play and then describe it to the group.

EXERCISE   SUMMARISING THE OUTPUT OF EXERCISES ON INTANGIBLES AND SERVICES

Example   summary of desirable intangibles and services identified

Desirable intangibles	Desirable service factors
Friendliness	Recruitment policy – recruit people who like other people. Ensure single person as customer's main point of contact.
Courtesy	Ensure all calls are answered within three rings. Train staff to give names clearly, remember please and thank you.
Prestige	Free gift of brand leader accessories. Other aspects of prestige to be dealt with via promotions.
Leading edge	The staff must be extremely knowledgeable.
Trustworthiness	Time guarantees. Compensation if a guarantee is not met.
Security	Performance guarantees. Financial guarantees.
Well-known	N/A The company's reputation must be established through media activity.

| Ethical | All employees should be trained in the company's ethical code. |
| Effective | Always deliver what we have promised to deliver. 100 per cent accurate paperwork 95+ per cent order fulfilment |

Note: Not all desirable intangibles can be tied to service standards.

Template   summary of desirable intangibles and services identified

Desirable intangibles	Desirable service factors

SUMMARY OF CHAPTER 4

If the new product is to be successful, it helps if it gives customers a good experience beyond its core function. The first challenge is to define the customer experience that the team wishes to develop and, as a by-product of that exercise, to establish service standards and desirable intangibles. This exercise may add impetus to existing products, which will reduce some of the risk associated with developing the new product.

5 *Variations on a theme*

Previous chapters have looked at the techniques which can be helpful in generating and then developing new product concepts. This chapter concentrates on the need for ideas about varying the product concept. Varying the product concept enables the organisation to offer a range of products to meet differing customer tastes; it also helps to extend the product life-cycle.

There are a number of aspects of the product concept which can be varied. Manufacturers are used to providing 'features and options' around a core product. In this review of the topic of variability we will also look at the potential for varying levels of service in line with a theory called 'diffusion of innovation', which has some overlaps with product life-cycle analysis. We will also consider the challenge of varying intangibles.

PRODUCT VARIATION – BASIC FEATURES

The first example is a very simple one. How many variations are there on the theme of 'a plastic container'? They may be infinite. Morphological analysis is a creativity technique developed by a Swiss researcher, Franz Zwicky. It is particularly helpful in exploring masses of variation. Key features of the product are listed in adjacent columns. To start with, *ad hoc* cutting and pasting of a typical stock list would be sufficient. The product development team can then choose new combinations of the attributes.

In the example given, three columns represent the key features of plastic containers. I have added the last column to help the new product development team to relate product possibilities to a potential use which may enable them to refine other variations.

For example, a container for use as a toolbox will have to be a certain size and it will also have to be stronger than a lunchbox. A container which is also a toy may need additional design and safety features.

Example morphological analysis

PLASTIC CONTAINERS Extracts from a typical stock list:			
Feature *Capacity (L)*	Feature *Shape*	Feature *Colour*	Use
0.5	Round	Blue	Storage (documents)
0.5	Conical	Clear	Measuring (liquids)
0.5	Square	Grey	Industrial (lubricants)
0.5	Rectangular	Red	Toy
1.0	Round	Yellow	Contain and display
1.0	Conical	White	Microwave cooking
1.0	Square	White	Deep-freeze storage
1.0	Rectangular	Blue	Beer making
1.0	Jug	Clear	Dairy
1.5	Round	Grey	Salad storage
1.5	Conical	Yellow	Rice storage
1.5	Square	Red	Pasta storage
1.5	Rectangular	Green	Lunchbox
2.0	Round	White	Fishing use (maggots?)
2.0	Conical	Clear	Presentation
and so on			

Template   morphological analysis

Feature 1	Feature 2	Feature 3	Use

The team can choose one attribute from each list to make up a container to suit each use in the final column. They may then evaluate the variations chosen on the basis of pre-set criteria, which may include originality and cost.

Example morphy evaluation

Use	Team's first choice	Team's second choice
measuring liquids	2l/jug/clear	5l/jug/clear
measuring solids	2l/square/clear	2l/conical/clear
deep-freeze storage	2l/rectangular/blue	2l/square/white
cassette box	1l/rectangular/clear + slots	2l/rectangular/blue
artist's materials	1l/oval/red + grid insert	2l/rectangular/yellow
hairdresser's box	5l/oval/blue + inserts	7l/rectangular/white
pet dishes	1l/round/red	2l/round/grey

Template   morphy evaluation

Use	Team's first choice	Team's second choice

The most important consideration is whether a variation can be justified on grounds of potential uses. Successful niche businesses have been built on just one product variation driven by a particular use. How many variations are there on a bag? Very many, but for years dancers have been carrying their tutus around in unflattering bin liners because ordinary bags on the market damaged their outfits. A nurse and a car salesman, whose daughter was keen on ballet, decided to design a bag for her. 'Showbags' is now a commercial venture, supported by Dewhurst Accessories, who produced some prototypes from sail fabric provided by another member of the 'Showbags' family. This company advised the couple to patent their idea and is now encouraging them to expand their product range – more variations on the theme of 'a bag'!

PRODUCT VARIATION – DIMENSIONS

Stanley Davis, in *Future Perfect* (1987), recommends the rethinking of three particular aspects of product in order to achieve innovative variation, if not breakthroughs. These three aspects are:

- **Time** – manufacturing time, service time, consumption time, idle time, speed of execution, speed of delivery. The variation of these aspects of time has led to just-in-time (or make-to-order) manufacturing, microwave cooking, fast food restaurants, time-share holidays, and 24-hour service, to name but a few.
- **Space** – size, shape, dimension, location. The variation of space has given us portables of many technologies and more esoteric concepts such as distance learning.
- **Mass** – density, texture, visibility, flexibility. The variation of mass is particularly applicable to the need to vary the strength or weight of a product according to its intended use.

Service products can also be subjected to most of this analysis, and generally they can be easily varied in terms of time and space.

EXERCISE   MORPHY USING *FUTURE PERFECT* CATEGORIES

The team can practise varying these key features. The following results came from an exercise including varying a 'meal' according to Davis's categories:

Example   morphy using *Future Perfect* categories: a meal

Feature: *Time*	Feature: *Space*	Feature: *Mass*	Use
Cooked to order	Tastefully decorated restaurant	Colourful garnish, items of food placed individually	Impress a business associate
Self-service	Café sporting easy-clean plastic furniture	food you feel/ hold, e.g. bananas, burgers	Feed a young child
Quick delivery service	At home	Lots of it!	Satisfy hunger whilst busy
and so on			

Template   morphy using *Future Perfect* categories

Feature *Time*	Feature *Space*	Feature *Mass*	Use

One of the driving forces of variation is to extend the product life-cycle. Attention to quality and design will dominate the development of a product during its introduction and growth phases. As it reaches maturity, variation assumes greater importance and may in fact delay saturation and decline. For example, baked beans have been a regular feature in American and British kitchen cupboards for many decades, but if we could travel back in time to the 1930s, we would probably think that the baked beans tasted quite different. That is because food manfacturers cater for changes in taste, changes in attitudes to food and changes in food processing techniques over the years. New recipes for baked beans come out quite often – thicker tomato sauce, less sugar, less salt, added tanginess, added vitamins, high fibre, etc.

Just as it is important to vary aspects of the core product throughout its life-cycle, service and intangibles also need to change as a product evolves.

PRODUCT VARIATION – SERVICES AND INTANGIBLES

Another approach to product variation which cannot be overlooked is the varying needs of customers throughout a product life-cycle for differing services and intangible values, as is shown in Figure 5.1

Whether or not core product variations are viable, a product can also be enhanced by variation in service levels and intangibles. Once again, these variations should reflect the fact that needs and tastes change subtly over time. The product life-cycle is a well-recognised concept and business professionals can appreciate the need for varying service options throughout a product's life. This consideration can be refined by also taking into account the diffusion of innovation curve. This concept is based on long-established research about customer attitudes and behaviour towards new products or services. Many high-technology companies segment their markets on the basis of diffusion of innovation. Taking the product life-cycle and the diffusion of innovation curve together will enable the product development team to design a comprehensive portfolio. The following customer groups have been identified and named according to their inclination to adopt new products or services:

Figure 5.1 The customer service curve, based on the product life-cycle and innovation curve

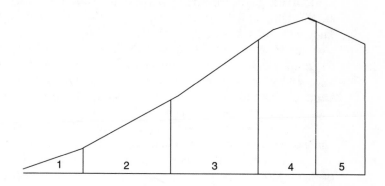

Stage 1 – Product introduction
– Personal service/ intangible of newness, being first
Stage 2 – Product growth
– Choice of services/ intangibles of leading edge and proven
Stage 3 – Product maturity
– Service commoditised/ intangibles of established solution, stability of provider
Stage 4 – Product saturation
– Telephone service + extended guarantees/ intangible of value for money
Stage 5 – Product decline
– Unique service available from niche third parties/ intangible of tradition

- 2.5 per cent innovators
- 13.5 per cent early adopters
- 34 per cent early majority
- 34 per cent late majority
- 16 per cent laggards

Innovators

Innovators are the customers a product or service needs just before
and just after it is launched. Whether it is a new widget or a new
work of art, innovators are the adventurous customers who will be
attracted to something by the intangible feature of its newness.
They want to go where no one has gone before, stretch boundaries,
bask in the white heat of discovery. They go to opening nights of
fringe plays, they try new cuisine and new fashion. They choose
unusual holiday destinations. Breweries in Britain have recently
attracted them to pubs by using curious names like 'The Rat and
Carrot' and 'The Orange Kipper'.

Consumer innovators are impulse buyers. They are risk-takers
and like excitement. Intangible products such as rollercoaster rides
are a case in point. Blackpool Pleasure Beach likes to keep ahead
of themepark trends, they open a major new 'white knuckles' ride
every four years. They host the Pepsi Max Big One, the tallest
rollercoaster in the world, which attracted 30 per cent more visitors
in its first year of operation. These visitors were the (predominantly young) people who wanted to say that they had been scared
to death on the Big One. Meanwhile, Blackpool Pleasure Beach
offers 144 other rides for the less adventurous.

In business-to-business markets, innovators base their company's competitive advantage on innovation and are keen to be beta
test sites for their supplier's latest technology. Joint projects or
partnerships are suitable arrangements for reducing the risk in their
leading-edge approach. They will, in any event, expect to be
lavishly attended by the best technical experts. Although their
own staff will be very accomplished, they will still expect high
service levels and the attention of the supplier's senior management. Innovators probably deserve such attention too, as once their
installation is successful and their competitive advantage assured,
they will probably act as reference sites. Gold-star service and the
intangible prestige of being first and being valued personally by
the supplier's chief executive are worthwhile investments. Innovators are noticeably the smallest group, and their approval is
critical to raising the interest of all the other groups. Satisfied
innovators will influence early adopters.

Early adopters

Early adopters are opinion leaders, in both business and consumer markets. They pride themselves on appreciating progress, but also on avoiding technological turkeys. They will go and see a new fringe play after it has had good reviews in the best newspapers or after friends have made favourable recommendations. They will try a new cuisine when the second restaurant opens up, or a new fashion once it breaks out of capital cities. They will book a new holiday destination once they are sure that the water and power supplies are secure. At work, they pride themselves on positive and cooperative relationships with suppliers, but keep an eye on the market too.

Intangibles of value to early adopters include the prestige of innovation but also assurance that it is proven. They may be interested in joint projects to some degree and will certainly be prepared to pay for extensive training and skills transfer so that they get the most out of their purchases. Service guarantees will be important, but they are unlikely to want to speak to the inventor directly.

This set of customers has extensive service needs, but they are probably willing to pay for the expertise the supplier's staff have gained supporting the innovators – at a premium price.

Early adopters expect to be valued by their suppliers, probably through status as a key account or in consumer markets via 'valued customer' mailings, such as those perfected by Reader's Digest. Early adopters nurse a product or service through its growth stage. They are strategically important to overall success.

Early majority

Buyers in the early majority would not see a new fringe play until it was on its second run in the larger regional theatres. They are somewhat risk-averse, but interested in adopting a product or service when it has moved beyond being proven and has become established. They may expect it to be easy to recruit staff who have experience of the innovation. They may expect basic services to be available from third parties. They would certainly be wary of being 'tied' to the manufacturer, but would also be seriously interested in the manufacturer's financial and technical stability. The early majority are active buyers in the product's maturity.

Support services can be a major challenge as accelerating numbers of a product are sold. Personal computer software packages are gaining complexity whilst their prices are falling, and they are more likely to be delivered to a user bundled with other manufacturers' products. Several leading software publishers responded to this development by introducing annual charges, or charges per call for premium support (support over and above standard free support). Lotus in the USA offers a variety of support options. Microsoft has encouraged third parties to provide support for its operating system NT.

There will be plenty of knowledge in the market about a mature product, and manufacturers would expect there to be rival service providers by this stage. The price of the supplier's service will come down, or it will be franchised out.

Late majority

Late majority customers, who are sometimes described as sceptical, adopt technology when it is in its saturation phase, as competition is fiercest and prices are beginning to drop. Reasonably, they expect a product that has already got so far not to need a great deal of service. Certainly, this is the time that most manufacturers turn their engineers' attention to new lines and work through third parties to repair and maintain older models. The pressure on cheapness for service delivery means that, by this stage, the telephone is overwhelmingly important. Carelines, helplines, advice lines and hotlines are all promoted.

There is an argument that customers do not appreciate service unless a high value is assigned to it. This approach has its dangers when a technology has moved into the saturation stage. Let's take the issue of parts/labour service agreements for white goods. Consumer programmes have slated white goods retailers for selling agreements at a very high price in relation to the value of goods acquired. Usually there is a manufacturer's agreement which is cheaper. However, since product quality has improved substantially over the past 20 years, customers might reasonably expect service agreements to be very cheap. Offering service, especially when there is minimal probability of having to provide it, looks like an easy route to a fatter profit line. Such tactics are always found out, and consumer campaigns lead to bad publicity and quite often to restrictive legislation. Creative thinking must be applied to providing meaningful services at acceptable prices.

Improvements to the product and its manuals mean that, by this stage, customers may not even be interested in buying support services.

Laggards

Some companies have played on traditional food, clothes, furniture and other goods to serve this niche, but usually consumers in this category are on low incomes, so it can be a difficult market. In some product areas, the demand for spares can sustain products which are still doing a satisfactory job way beyond their natural life-cycle. In business-to-business markets there are many good reasons for being a laggard, and the most important one is the disruption that change can wreak. Companies are slow to adopt technology when they have older systems that are working perfectly adequately and when the investment involved in change would threaten cash flow. Sometimes, staff are unwilling to change.

By this stage, customers will have difficulty finding service providers, apart from a few specialists in 'dog' technology and the supplier of the original equipment. Any service requirement for nearly obsolete skills might command a high asking price.

Summary of the service/intangibles life-cycle variations

Product life-cycle stage	Customer type, by diffusion of innovation	Service levels	Intangibles
Introduction	Innovators	High – personal service from experts	Newness, being first
Growth	Early adopters	Choice service from supplier	Leading edge + proven
Maturity	Early majority	Commoditised	Established solution, supplier stability
Saturation	Late majority	Telephone-based or other low-price options	Value for money
Decline	Laggards	Unique	Tradition

SUMMARY OF CHAPTER 5

Product variation is usually hailed as an ideal way to extend a product's life-cycle, but it is also a route into niche markets or a way of revitalising replacement markets. The need for variation in the core product offering is greater as a product matures, and variation using themes of time, space and mass can provoke considerable innovation. Services and intangibles ought also to be varied over the product life-cycle in order to suit changing customer needs.

6 Product strategy development

The first part of this chapter discusses aspects of the marketing mix that complement 'product', the other 'P's of marketing. In the latter part of the chapter, morphological analysis is used to bring the different 'P's together to provide suites of intangibles.

OTHER ASPECTS OF THE MARKETING MIX

To the customer, there is only one 'P' in the marketing mix, product. The other 'P's which exercise the minds of marketing strategists are, to the customer, intangible aspects of the big 'P'. In this chapter the different aspects of the marketing mix are examined as if they were features of the product. Then morphological analysis is applied so that the product development team can make decisions about the appropriate intangibles for the new product.

In order to prioritise strategies, a review of the customer's critical success factors is required. This indicates where immediate focus is necessary, but the long term must also be considered. Aspects of the marketing mix can assume varying importance throughout the life-cycle of a product, and this challenge will be considered at the end of the chapter.

Place/channels and processes

Wherever you are in the market map shown in Figure 6.1, you must consider how other players in the market affect the customer's experience of your product. How do you work with distributors and retailers to add value? How do you work 'upstream' with suppliers to add value? Could you market directly to customers rather than selling on to distributors/retailers? If so, how – by

Figure 6.1 Place/channels and progress

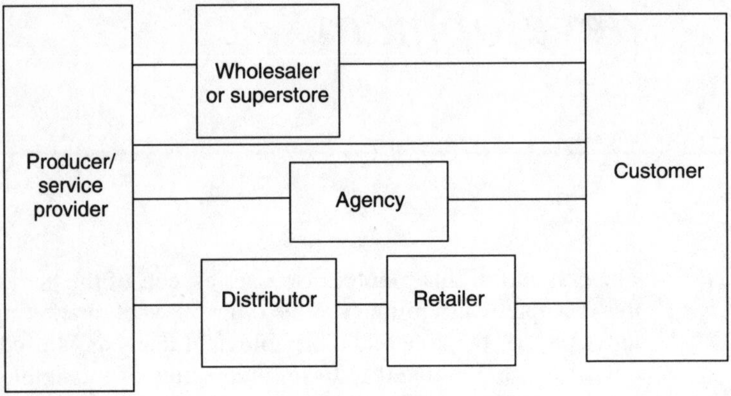

visit, telephone, mail? Consumers, and some business buyers, have become accustomed to a choice of purchasing venue. In particular, there is a revival of shopping methods which save the consumer time, such as mail order. Technology can offer new 'place' opportunities; electronic shopping is beginning to take off. This trend is helpful to the manufacturer who wants to develop 'consumer pull' by a direct approach.

A manufacturer's desire to 'own' its relationship with the ultimate consumer is not necessarily unfair to other parties in the value chain. Brokers used to be all-powerful in the insurance industry; consumers relied on their recommendation. Along came insurers who wanted direct contact with the customer. Now brokers are more likely to work in partnership with insurance companies to mutually add value and provide for consumers looking for a more personal service or who represent a more unusual risk.

Even food manufacturers are starting to build relationships with consumers via direct mail. In the 1980s, retailers extended their brand from the overall shopping experience to food products themselves, thereby presenting a threat to manufacturers' brands.

Manufacturers therefore had to move the place in which the brand preference is made from the shelf, which the retailer controls, to the consumer's dinner table, where they can enjoy a free sample in splendid isolation from the shopping experience.

In industry-to-industry marketing some suppliers of raw materials concentrate account management effort on the end-user company rather than the company that acts as mixer or assembler.

'Place' is not just a matter of the location at which a customer meets the product, it is also the effectiveness of the process which gets it there. A company's overall ability to deliver its product by maintaining effective relationships throughout the supply chain is becoming increasingly important. Supply chain management is a key area of competitiveness. American retailer Wal-mart attributes much of its success – profit margins twice what its competitors can make – to efficient in-bound logistics. The company can get products onto its shelves more quickly than competitors, and therefore it has a much higher stock turnover.

Many manufacturing companies have copied the Japanese practice of partnership sourcing, working with preferred suppliers to take cost and inefficiencies out of the process of delivering value to the customer. This is vital, given that the consumer of the 1990s seeks more and more value. Getting everyone in the supply chain working together to eliminate costs requires a great deal of trust, which takes time to build up. In the meantime, the product development team can draw up lists of internal process improvements which could be made. Good products deserve efficient administration processes to get them to customers and to support customers' service requirements.

There are two very good reasons for innovation in distribution. First, distribution can be very costly. Distribution absorbs 30 per cent of the cost of a new car, and for some goods the share is 50 per cent. Second, the lifestyles and work practices of customers favour more direct delivery of what they want. Use of the telephone and electronic mail have reached from business-to-business markets into consumer markets. In fact, faster exchange on information seems to be the key to reducing distribution costs.

One American clothing company's strategy is simply to be second to market, but to apply high technology to distribution. This approach is highly profitable. VF's clothing is described as 'workaday', but VF is a market leader in computerised market response systems. That means their lines are always in stock at popular retailers like Wal-Mart and J. C. Penney. VF supplies tens of thousands of retailers with hundreds of styles, efficiently, and with a partnership approach. VF's speedy replenishment of popular items helps the retailer to make money too. They get more of what the customer wants and less of what does not sell well.

Business process redesign has opened up whole new debates about customer focus.

EXERCISE   BRAINSTORMING – WHAT PLACE?

The product development team should now brainstorm all the places where a customer might meet the new product with a view to buy. Apply the SCAMPER checklist, especially reversal – perhaps the team can come up with a new route to market!

After the brainstorm, the team may wish to review the list and eliminate the locations which are obviously unsuitable, although they must take care not to eliminate 'intermediate impossibles'. Consideration should be given to the way in which a location influences the buying decision, such as 'because it is here, I know it must be good value'; 'because it is here, I know I am taking a calculated risk'; 'because it is here, I know I will receive excellent professional help to make the most of it'. The team must also consider the process involved in serving locations and whether it suits the company's capabilities.

Promotion

Promotion is solely concerned with communicating relevant messages and impressions to the relevant audiences.

(Christopher and McDonald, 1985)

Even if a company already has a positive image and a reputation for quality products, promotion still has to be handled with care. The objectives of promotions must be clear. The effect of promotions on product intangibles must be thought through. Good promotions cannot make up for weak products, but bad promotions can spoil the potential of good products. Promotions should draw the attention of relevant decision-makers to the product in a way that respects both the decision-makers and the products themselves.

The importance of matching the right promotion to the right product becomes abundantly clear when it goes wrong. When panic sets in to a sales force, as it can do in recessionary times, salespeople know that discounts and 'give-aways' will provide an easy short-term answer to the sales dip. Unfortunately, they make the profits dip through the floor. The Hoover free flights promotion was a classic case.

It is rare when a brand name takes a dominant role in the English language. 'Hoover' was such a rare case, making it into the *Oxford Dictionary* as a colloquial term for cleaning the carpet with a vacuum cleaner. The 'hoover' may be an Electrolux. 'To hoover' or 'to do the hoovering' show the noun used as a verb, and one might even hear a carpet referred to as 'well-hoovered'.

For 50 years in Britain 'Hoover' was inextricably associated with what the product did for its owner. Until, in 1992, the Hoover name was repeatedly uttered in the same breath as 'free flights fiasco'.

In 1992, Hoover started offering free flights to Europe or the USA to purchasers of Hoover vacuum cleaners worth more than £100. Sales promotion specialists were baffled – how could it make sense to offer a promotional gift worth two or three times the price of the product? Demand for free flights was high, therefore many Hoover hoovers were bought. Hoover could not cope with their new role as Good Fairy travel agents, and their American parent Maytag had to step in and set up a task force of 250 people to sort out the mess. By 1994, Hoover was still facing legal actions in small claims courts throughout the UK, and in the High Court. The company was also being investigated by the Advertising Standards Authority on several counts.

Where did Hoover go wrong? Well, the advertisements placed by Hoover emphasised the free flights rather than their own doughty product – the Hoover hoover. Advertising professionals say that in the realistic 1990s, promotions are more successful if they communicate integral values, fundamental products' truths, such as the creaminess of a beer or the tanginess of a sausage. Added emotional values are also important. Hoover ignored these rules and the promotion attracted people who wanted to buy holidays, not people who wanted to buy vacuum cleaners, and the take-up far exceeded any previous free flights offer by other companies. A smaller company would have been bankrupted.

Another trend observed by the advertising profession is that creative promotions save money. By creative promotions they do not mean surreal television advertisements. Midland Bank and Guinness found that their series of surreal ads on UK television merely confused people. Creative promotions do add impact by being different, but they must still be comprehendable. The following examples come from recent UK advertising effectiveness awards:

- A Scottish health club that targeted the unfit and overweight
- The Co-operative Bank for differentiating themselves on ethics
- A brewery that led its brand in magazine advertising rather than TV
- A sweet manufacturer that promoted a new chocolate bar entirely on local radio, rather than TV.

These campaigns were all very effective, and most were cheaper than the traditional promotional route for their product types. Alternative media also include:

- Advertisements on eggs (a message in vegetable dye is sprayed on to the eggshell). I have never eaten an egg with an ad on it, but I did read some of the press coverage when BT chose this method to raise awareness of reduced call rates!
- Liveried taxis – United Airlines have paid for 170 London black cabs to be painted half in yellow New-York style, sporting the slogan 'The best of both worlds'.

■ The tops of buses – this is how *The Economist* advertises to professionals in their high-rise offices in the City of London.

Agencies advise clients not to be too frivolous about innovative advertising; many target customers like their preferred brand to be 'serious'. Promotions do have to add intangible value to the product. If a promotion gives anything away, it must do so for the sole purpose of taking the customer beyond awareness to long-term preference. Try-and-buy promotions are effective in these terms. Samples of a new tomato sauce might tempt loyal customers of another brand to switch, and that would be more cost-effective than hours of TV advertising. 'Try and buy' also works in the business environment. It worked famously for Post-it notes and is widely used for software and computer services.

EXERCISE   PROMOTIONS BRAINSTORM

> The product development team should now brainstorm all the promotions which might raise customer awareness about the new product. Apply the SCAMPER checklist. As a follow-up to the brainstorm the team could come up with some analogies for promotion. In nature, peacocks provide a colourful display to attract peahens. Other animals dance or sing for their mates. Flowers use scent to attract pollinating insects. Analogy can help to add options to the list.
>
> The team should now eliminate the obviously unsuitable, but should also 'murder-board' the promotions which are most common for this type of product. If the product would usually be promoted by TV advertising, the team should list all the things they hate about TV advertising. The 'accepted' route to market does not necessarily deserve a place on the list.

The other 'P' – people

> You can't provide a good customer service if your employees
> are miserable.
> (Jeffrey Pfeffer, Stanford Business School quoted by Richard
> Donkin in the *Financial Times*, 8/2/95)

'People' is not one of the famous four 'P's of marketing (Product,
Price, Place, Promotion). However, in an increasing number of
cases, clients are putting a 'people' section into their marketing
plan – it is the *de facto* fifth P. A company's people qualities can
enhance products. Products presented by or supported by demor-
alised and depressed people are tarnished. It seems more important
than ever in these days of increasing consumer sophistication to
treat 'people policies' as part of the marketing mix.

So many product intangibles rely on people, and innumerable
words have been written about the importance of delighting
employees as well as customers. Yet a recent government-
commissioned survey indicates that the labour market is returning
to the conditions of the early nineteenth century. The decline in
trade union membership in the developed world has not resulted
in any increase in alternative forms of consultation or best
practice in human resource management. In fact, the report
claimed that management was increasingly autocratic, treating
employees as 'factors of production'.

A fearful atmosphere is widely acknowledged to inhibit human
creativity, and it also costs organisations money in lost productivity. High-level newspaper reports publicising research about the
costs of work-place stress, not to mention court cases, do not yet
seem to have resulted in widespread changes in policy. It is
remarkable that any company can ignore the evidence in favour
of positive 'people' policies.

If corporate culture is abrasive, it can also lead to embarrass-
ment as fearful employees extend the culture out towards customers. The results include everything from inappropriate selling, a
widespread problem in the financial services industry in the UK in
the 1980s, to 'dirty tricks' against competitors which end up in the
courts, as in Virgin's case against British Airways. Virgin's
complaint is that BA staff tried to poach Virgin's transatlantic

passengers. If, on the other hand, employee morale and employee benefits matter to management, the results can be dramatic.

ISS is a world-wide cleaning company with its headquarters in Denmark. They have the challenging of motivating staff in an industry where wage rates are usually low and where winning price-sensitive contracts is a critical success factor. ISS worked out that high staff turnover rates were costing the company dearly. They now have unique recruitment and retention policies, including a high level of staff training. At Heathrow Airport, smartly uniformed, well-paid ISS cleaners are able to give the airport's customers information about the location of departure gates, or the Harrods store. The company supports the concept of a minimum wage and union membership.

Jeffrey Pfeffer of Stanford's Business School researched the five top-performing US companies between 1972 and 1992. All of these companies recognised unions as well as offering better job security, better wages and better employee share options than their rivals. Pfeffer has demonstrated that companies that pay close attention to the needs of their work-forces have achieved exceptional economic returns in competitive industries. A low-paid, low-morale work-force is not cost-effective in the long run.

EXERCISE ROLE-PLAY

Volunteers are required in the team to role-play the following sample situations:

- Team member 1 is a customer in a hurry. She has received a mailing from Company X about their new printer. She calls the number given for more information and, although gushingly polite, the telesales clerk, played by team member 2, cannot answer her questions. How do the characters feel when they put the telephone down?
- Team member 3 is a skilled manual worker and a responsible community representative with good contacts in the local press. He witnesses a young manager shouting at his secretary about an appointment with a customer that she had booked for the wrong day. What does he do next?

> What does the young manager do to retrieve the situation with the disappointed customer?
>
> ■ Team member 4 plays the Super Sales Representative. His formidable record has come to the attention of the company's arch-competitor, who makes him an attractive financial offer. He knows that his customers will be disappointed if he goes, but he is embarrassed because his employer has been vilified in the national press for sudden redundancies whilst board members had recently voted themselves large rises. What does he do? Given that a change in their main contact is a brand switching point for many customers, what does the company do if he asks to leave?

These scenarios are intended to test assumptions.

■ We know customers are frustrated when they cannot get information, but we must also consider the state of mind of the clerk, who has not been empowered to give information.

■ We know managers are unlikely to throw a tantrum and assign blame to others in front of their boss, but what happens when they display inappropriate behaviour in front of an employee with wider influence? First of all, what message does it give other employees and how might they be tempted to use it? Second, does it help to resolve the problem with the customer if blame has been assigned?

■ The third scenario plays to management's worst fear – losing key staff. How are key staff affected by negative people policies? They may not leave because of them, but such policies might well influence a go/stay decision.

BRINGING IT ALL TOGETHER USING MORPHOLOGICAL ANALYSIS

If we treat the elements of 'the marketing mix' as features of product, and try to mix and match them using morphological analysis, interesting combinations can be drawn up which create intangibles for the product. For the purpose of the initial exercise, consideration of the price 'P' has been deferred to later in the chapter.

EXERCISE MORPHOLOGICAL ANALYSIS – THE MARKETING MIX

From the earlier exercises, the team will have lists of places, promotions and people to enter in the columns. Now they have to put together some combinations which would complement the new product. The idea of the exercise is to open up discussion about a wide selection of possible combinations before evaluating their feasibility.

Feature *Place*	Feature *Promotion*	Feature *People*
Home/mail	TV advertising	Telesales rep
Department store (town)	Magazine ad – local	Researcher
Warehouse	Newspaper ad – local	Shop assistant
Business premises	Posters – main road	Professional rep
Out-of-town mall	Direct mail	Computer operator
Street market	Telemarketing	Order entry clerk
Factory outlet	Samples	Shop owner/manager
Place of work	Money-off coupon	Demonstrator
Home/visit	Street megaphone	Franchisee
Supermarket	Sandwich board	Temporary cashier
Village hall	On-shelf display	Sub-contractor
Van on street corner	Word of mouth	Account manager
Neighbourhood shop	Pavement A-board	Friend/relative
Business/visit	Discount	Market trader
Business/fax or e-mail	Press coverage	Mature shop assistant
Home/catalogue	Advertorial	Self
Home/telephone	Eggshell ads	Shop assistant
Business/visit	Window display	Networking contact

Template   marketing mix – morphy table

Place	Promotion	People

EVALUATING THE 'P'S AS PRODUCT ATTRIBUTES

Whilst the overall level of desired margin is bound to be an evaluation factor, remember that many companies are successful by delivering their products to a wide range of customers in a variety of ways which return different margins. The team must also consider qualitative factors. Degree of innovation in the approach might be one such factor. The team should also choose at least one other factor which will sum up the complement to the product, such as prestige, simplicity, high-tech, homeliness, etc.

The chosen combinations can be scored by team members individually and then aggregated or the team can try and discuss scorings in open forum.

Example   marketing mix morphy evaluation chart

Combination	Profitability	Innovation	Homeliness	Total
Home visit/ sample/friend	5	4	9	18
Home mail/ sample/postman	9	4	5	18

Neighbourhood shop/on-shelf display/shop owner	7	3	7	17
Village hall/ sample/researcher	5	4	6	15
Supermarket/ local radio ad/ demonstrator	6	4	5	15
Home/eggshell ad/ self (?)	8	9	7	24
Van on street corner/A-board / demonstrator	7	5	5	17
Home TV/TV ad/telesales (freephone number)	6	3	6	15

There is a runaway winner in this example, with a number of other options clustered some way behind. A combination of these second-placed approaches, phased over time, could follow on from the initial introductory method and support the product in its growth stage.

Template   marketing mix morphy evaluation chart

Combination	Profitability	Innovation	Other	Total

Although we can make assumptions about the profitability of a marketing mix, there is a constraint. Price is determined by external rather than internal factors.

PRICE

The final 'P' to consider is price. When I was first introduced to economics (in the 1970s), I was taught that there are two types of pricing strategies that can be applied to new products before the forces of supply and demand start to demonstrate what the price should be. Products could be introduced with a high skimming price, which would limit demand whilst production was being geared up, or they could be introduced with a low penetration price which would ensure high volumes quickly and secure a foothold in the market. By the mid-1980s it seemed as if there was no such thing as a penetration price, skimming prices were preferred, and they did not come down very much as the product matured. The Filofax was very much a product of the 1980s – a new and expensive diary concept which became very popular. However, even the cheap copies were not all that cheap compared to the obvious substitute, a humble diary.

There is one thing that we can be sure of in the 1990s. Price is no longer about status, it is about value. This is described by market researchers as a long-term shift in attitude. It is well accepted in marketing that a good product should command a premium price, but several years of recession have made consumers canny and marketers must respond to their demands. As the *Sunday Times* reported in January 1995:

Once it was fashionable to drop hints about how MUCH one had spent . . . the mid-1990s consumer . . . prefers to let it slip just how LITTLE their new purchase cost them. These days, the department store seems more like the souk, so widespread is the haggling.

For example, British retailers in the 1980s enjoyed the highest margins in Europe, and charged prices up to 30 per cent higher than their US counterparts. So, European and US retailers saw the opportunity to set up in the UK and compete on price. Due to the 'mercilessly low prices' in new German and Scandinavian discount stores and American warehouse clubs, supermarket prices in the UK are falling. They reduced by 18 per cent between 1992 and 1995. British retailers now have more modest profits.

EXERCISE PORTER'S FIVE FORCES

One way of estimating how much pressure there will be on the price of a new product is to examine competitive forces in the market. After that, market research should be conducted to check customers' price expectations.

The concept of five competitive forces in a market was introduced by Harvard strategist Michael Porter. The forces are:

$$\text{Ease of entry to the market}$$
$$\Downarrow$$
$$\text{Power of suppliers} \Rightarrow \begin{array}{c} \text{Number/strength} \\ \text{of competitors} \end{array} \Leftarrow \text{Power of consumers}$$
$$\Uparrow$$
$$\text{Availability of substitutes}$$

Consider each of the five forces and how they affect each of your target market segments for this new product.

- Ease of entry to the market
  Does it require huge capital investment to produce this kind of product, or can anyone set up in their garage? If it is easy to enter the market, count this competitive pressure as HIGH. If you only expect entry from an eccentric multi-millionaire, count it as LOW.
- Power of suppliers
  Are there only a few suppliers of the raw materials you need, or are the suppliers in some kind of protective association (such as OPEC)? If so, this competitive pressure is high. If you can get supplies anywhere, it is low.
- Number and strength of competitors
  If you are the brand leader and your competitors are a few also rans, this competitive pressure is low. If there are lots of

healthy companies vying for brand leadership, the pressure is high.

■ Power of customers
If you are selling to millions of consumers, they might still be knowledgeable and organised enough to exert power in the marketplace, especially in a recession. If consumers are powerful, this competitive pressure is high. The ultimate example of lack of power of consumers is the case of addictive drugs – once hooked, the customer is helpless. Even so, suppliers cannot be complacent. Years of health education have dramatically reduced the number of people in the developed world who are addicted to nicotine.

■ Availability of substitutes
If the price of coffee is high, people may drink tea. If there are a lot of substitutes for your product, this competitive pressure is high. If your offering is unique, it is low. Regard the option to do nothing as a substitute too, it is often a tempting one for the customer!

Example   five forces: new washing powder

Force	Rating
Ease of entry into the market: Some small companies have succeeded on ecology ticket, but in general the investment required is prohibitive.	L
Power of suppliers: There are only a few chemical companies in the world who can supply ingredients.	H
Number/strength of competitors: This market is generally regarded as a duopoly, but brands are threatened by supermarket 'own label'.	M
Power of customers: Customers used to be passive, but are applying pressure on ecological and ethical issues.	M

Availability of substitutes: Few. People like to keep clothes clean using modern methods.	L
Overall	MEDIUM

It is easy enough to deduce an overall score from the balance of high/low/medium scores in the five categories. In this example, we have two medium and two low, but one high cancelling out one low score and leaving the weight in the medium category. Even when competitive forces are high, companies still have to take risks with new products, but a low entry price might be advisable.

Template   five forces

Force	Rating
Ease of entry into the market:	
Power of suppliers:	
Number/strength of competitors:	
Power of customers:	
Availability of substitutes:	
Overall	

FINISHING TOUCHES

The only way to develop overall product strategy further is to do so with the power derived from customer feedback. Most companies continually conduct customer research to see how they compare with nearest competitors. Even with a creative marketing mix, a market research check will demonstrate where most emphasis is required.

The first list in the critical success factors (CSF) analysis table contains the factors about a product offering that the customers regard as important to them. It should not be too long a list, the top six factors is the recommended maximum. Customers weight or rank these factors according to their relative value to them, and then score the company or brand under which the product will be launched. The competitor's score will be that of the 'best in class' supplier/brand chosen by the customers. If 'ourco' is the best in class, then the competitor's score will be the next in class. Multiplying scores by weight gives an indication of which aspects of the product will need most investment in the introductory stage.

Example   analysis of critical success factors

Critical Success Factors	Weight	Ourco score	weight x score	Best comp'tor score	weight x score
Quality	30	7	210	9	270
Price	20	9	180	8	160
Image	10	6	60	9	90
Delivery	10	4	40	7	70
Personal service	30	8	240	7	210
Totals			730		800

This example shows that in the near future the company must concentrate on improving product quality, so often a function of the processes in the organisation, as indeed is the low score for delivery. Since image is also lagging behind the best of breed competitor, once the process issue has been addressed, the company should invest in promotion.

Template   strategic priorities

Critical Success Factor	Weight	Ourco score	weight x score	Best comp'tor score	weight x score

That is the near future sorted out. What about the long term?

STRATEGY ADJUSTMENTS THROUGHOUT THE PRODUCT LIFE-CYCLE

The 'P's vary in importance throughout the product life-cycle. It depends on the type of product, but the following example is not unusual:

Example   the four 'P's in the product life-cycle – mapping strategy variations

Life-cycle position	Place	Promotion	Price	People
Pre-launch	Alpha/beta test (customer premises)	Enigmatic build-up + word of mouth	Research required	Technical specialists delivering service
Introduction	Customer premises	WOW! RA-RA!	Adjust according to take-up	Product champions and account managers

Growth	Roll out through third-party showrooms	Still investing	Stabilise	Highly trained sales reps
Maturity	Reliance on more third-party retail outlets	Declining budgets/ joint promos	Stabilise	Sales assistant in shop, telesales/ service support staff in manufacturer
Saturation	Direct mail	Low budget mailings/ catalogue	Reduce, or add things to the product offering	Telephone sales assistant
Decline	Discount warehouses	None	Discount to clear stocks	Storesman

The overall investment in the other 'P's peaks in the growth period. Price warrants little attention after the growth period, whilst expenditure on training third-party's staff is still high. Choice of place and people is most critical in the maturity and saturation phases.

Fashion products go through product life-cycle stages very quickly, and are a good example of this model at work. A lot of hype precedes a top designer's new collection, then it is launched with a lavish show and made available to opinion-leader customers. The designs are rolled out to exclusive stores, then to department stores and, before fashion laggards can get round to buying them, they are in special warehouse sales and then gone, *passé*.

Some products have been around for such a long time that it is difficult to tell what phase of the product life-cycle they are in. Some technologies, such as computers, seem to be in more than one stage at once. Entrants with a new variation on the product offering can still find opportunities to gain market share. For example, in the developed world, despite the requirement for new models, the internal combustion engine as a means of personal transport is in its saturation phase. The big-name manufacturers communicate with prospective customers by direct mail, whilst car dealers, who had been tied to one manufacturer in the past, are now pursuing a supermarket approach, with a range of competing brands on offer on their forecourts.

A new player, such as Daewoo of Korea, has to do something special in order to win customers. They have decided to offer extra service to car buyers and to promote their whole product offering through an 'extra-service' location – their own family-friendly retail outlets.

Template   the four 'P's in the product life-cycle – mapping strategy variations

Life-cycle position	Place	Promotion	Price	People
Pre-launch				
Introduction				
Growth				
Maturity				
Saturation				
Decline				

SUMMARY OF CHAPTER 6

All aspects of the marketing mix are important, but the others are nothing without product. If the other 'P's of the marketing mix are perfect, but the product is poor, failure will ensue. A product that meets customers' needs and delivers competitive advantage is the first priority of customer focus.

The argument of this chapter is that other aspects of the marketing mix should be treated as features of the product offering. The customer perceives product intangibles in the place where it is sold, its price, the way in which it is promoted and the qualities of the person who sells it. A good product deserves excellent, appropriate marketing strategies to support it. Team effort should be devoted to designing the marketing mix as part of the product-for-market offering and to applying investment to customers' immediate priorities. In the longer term, a wider variety of approaches can be accommodated and costs rationalised.

7 Implementation issues – risk assessment and contingencies

> Strategy must go with the army to the field in order to arrange particulars on the spot, and to make the modifications in the general plan which incessantly become necessary in war. Strategy can therefore never take its hand from the work for a moment.
>
> (Clausewitz, 1832)

We have now thoroughly determined our product – what need it fulfils, what is its core function, its surround and the marketing mix which will make it successful. We have strategy, now we have to take it down to the field of battle.

This chapter looks at the issues to be considered before and during product strategy implementation. It is based on recent research into the wide variety of risks involved in introducing new products, and provides the structure for a day-long implementation workshop. Before significant sums of money are invested in converting product concepts into product launches, creative criticism must be applied. The topics listed below have to be discussed by the new product development team, perhaps with some guests from senior management in the meetings. The team will also be aware of the need to revisit some of the topics during the course of development, as circumstances impacting the business environment change so quickly.

- Strategic fit
- Product advantage
- Market opportunity
- Quantitative success

■ Ethics
■ Resource constraints
■ Project planning
■ Marketing risks
■ Technical risks

The proof of a strategy is in the implementation. Implementation planning involves not just a schedule of interdependent actions, but assessment of risks and preparation of contingencies. The military analogy is very suitable. Clausewitz (1832) explains that, in combat, it is essential to be alive to the possibility of unforeseen events. At the simplest level, if the enemy's tactics are concealed by woods or hills, it is obvious that more than one plan of attack must be anticipated. According to the degree of uncertainty, strategic reserves must be prepared to fulfil contingency plans.

From time to time, high risks have to be taken. Teams can succeed with high-risk projects if they have explored the problems, are prepared for them and are still convinced of the feasibility of the endeavour. In Clausewitz's terms:

> Boldness, directed by an overruling intelligence, is the stamp of the hero: this boldness does not consist in venturing directly against the nature of things. . . . The more boldness lends wings to the mind and the discernment, so much the farther they will reach in their flight . . . but certainly always only in the sense that with greater objects, greater dangers are connected.

There are many detailed volumes on how to avoid product failure. The purpose of this chapter is to introduce inhibitors to product strategy success and to suggest how creativity techniques can be applied to circumvent or minimise them.

There are two diagrams which are particularly helpful when looking at each of the categories in this chapter. The first, Figure 7.1, is called a force field analysis:

Figure 7.1 Force field analysis

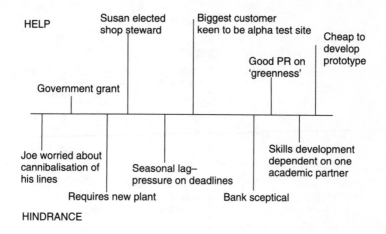

In almost every aspect of 'implementability' there will be factors that help and factors which hinder. Some may be a small help, in which case a short vertical line can be drawn above the horizontal; other will be a big help, in which case a longer line is drawn. Lines drawn below the horizontal indicate the degree of hindrance. The force field analysis is a pictorial representation of the group's 'gut feeling'. Its use ensures that all the things which enthuse the optimists and all the things which worry the pessimists can be brought together and balanced. Even if there are more hindrance factors than help factors, it does not necessarily mean that a product concept is not worth pursuing. Some of the best technology invented within companies has faced a battle for internal acceptance.

The force field analysis serves the purpose of managing expectations. In implementation workshops it is advisable to assign the role of devil's advocate. If senior managers are attending, they are ideal candidates for this role. If there are to be no nasty surprises in the execution of a good idea, every potential problem must be flushed out in advance. The next stage of analysis is to assess

Figure 7.2 Impact and probability scales

IMPACT

	high		low
high	select a best solution and work through a contingency plan	raise awareness, make note of obvious solutions	
low	raise awareness, make note of obvious solutions	list, but do not action	

PROBABILITY

whether or not a contingency plan is required. This process is illustrated by Figure 7.2.

IMPLEMENTATION ISSUES

The categories described here are based on extensive Ph.D. research conducted by Steve Cook (1994) of the Cranfield Centre for Advanced Technology in Marketing.

Corporate fit

One aspect of success which ought to top the chronological list of product reviews is establishing that the product strategy is in line with corporate image and mission. Unless your company has set out to be a conglomerate, diversification is widely considered to be the highest risk strategic option. Because of this acknowledged risk, troubleshooter Sir John Harvey-Jones frequently advises companies featured on his television programmes to 'stick to your knitting'. 'Sticking to your knitting' does not mean stagnation. If an organisation's mission is to fulfil identifiable customer needs, innovation can still be dramatic.

In the nineteenth century, the railway was a revolution in travel. Railway companies were hugely successful. However, in the twentieth century, railway companies stuck to running railways and eventually died. Had they seen their mission as fulfilling people's need to get from A to B, they might have developed buses and cars as well.

Nevertheless, introducing radically new technology will not necessarily be easy, even if it does fit in with corporate image, because it could still challenge customers' perceptions of corporate image. Even rebellious stars of popular music have problems when they want to develop their repertoire. Bob Dylan became famous for singing protest songs to an acoustic guitar and mouth organ. When he experimented with an electric guitar his followers were outraged.

EXERCISE   SCENARIO PLANNING

A creative technique which could be applied when checking corporate fit is scenario-building. In addition to a guest from senior management, the group would also benefit from the views of a guest from the shop floor whose perceptions of corporate culture might be quite different. External interpreters of the company's image, such as a partnership supplier or customer are also important.

Warm up for this exercise by asking the participants to talk about a fashionable product or service that they remember from their youth, either a failure or a success. Now imagine your company in twenty or more years from now. Speculate about the future business environment, how customer tastes will have developed, and who the competitors will be. By then, your product will be history. How will it be remembered?

Example   scenario planning

	Scenario 1	Scenario 2	Scenario 3	Scenario 4
Politics/ legislation	nationalist dictatorship	social democracy	conservatism	regional hegemony
Economy	Command economy, emphasis on infrastructure and defence	Mixed economy, support for public and manufacturing sectors	Squeeze on public sector, emphasis on services	Joint ventures between big corporations in trading bloc, exclusion of some external investment
Social trends/tastes	Increasingly home-centred purchasing and entertainment	Early retireds have increasing consumer power	Decline in popularity of credit, more savings	Emigration to warmer/ more prosperous parts of the trading bloc
Technology	Technical means of social control receive investment	Health, computer-assisted education	Market for advances in entertainment and security products	Locally produced technology extensions, intra-bloc networks

EXERCISE DEBATE

> If the outcome of this future scenario looks too rosy, conduct a debate (using all the proper rules of debate) between two members of the team, one acting as an extreme product romantic, the other acting as an extreme cynic. The team will have to make contributions and vote at the end. Who wins? If the romantic is heavily defeated, then the product concept ought to go back to the drawing board.

Template scenario planning

	Scenario 1	Scenario 2	Scenario 3	Scenario 4
Politics/ legislation				
Economy				
Social trends/ tastes				
Technology				

Product advantage

Product advantage also has to be confirmed. This ought to be done at an early stage in development, when altering the specification can be done cheaply, but also repeatedly checked to avoid 'drift'. Earlier chapters have discussed the application of creativity techniques to functional development, checking with market research, prototyping and alpha/beta testing. Common sense dictates that if a new product's advantage is merely superficial, customers may well stick with the established solution.

Researchers Cooper and Kleinschmidt (1987) discovered that common sense does not always prevail in rarefied corporate environments. They reported that many new products are 'me-too' (or provide a technical feature of no relevance to the customer). They concluded that five out of seven major components of market impact are associated with product advantage, which they describe as the dominant factor in success. The product development team should brainstorm to create a list of all the aspects of product superiority, product quality, unique benefits, problem-solving and use of advanced technology that their concept delivers. As a sanity check, ask a different multi-disciplinary team to do the same – are they so convinced? The bravest teams will also ask another team to 'murder-board'!

This emphasis on product advantage does not preclude continuous improvement. The first drill manufacturer to provide the same drills as last year but with longer leads and integral plugs was meeting four out of five of Cooper and Kleinschmidt's criteria – apparently minor changes can deliver dramatic improvements in superiority, quality, uniqueness and problem solving.

EXERCISE   BRAINSTORM PRODUCT ADVANTAGES

Check Cooper and Kleinschmidt's criteria:

■ Product superiority
■ Quality
■ Uniqueness
■ Problem solving
■ Use of advanced technology

Check the output of the product development team with another team.

In order to assess major criticisms as well as the accumulation of positives, ask a third team to murder-board the product using Cooper and Kleinschmidt's criteria.

Market opportunity

It has to be accepted that minor changes provide only short windows of market opportunity, since it is easy for competitors to follow suit. By using brainstorming and morphological analysis regularly, and by rewarding suggestions from all corners of the company, customers and suppliers, a product development team should have enough raw material to accelerate the pace of minor improvements on existing products. Constantly keeping one small step ahead of the opposition will command customers' respect over time. In 1994 3M were reported to have raised their well-known target of 25 per cent of sales to come from products less than 5 years old to 30 per cent of sales to come from products less than 4 years old – all in aid of keeping ahead of the pace of change expected by 1990s' customers.

Quantum leaps can command world respect instantly, but they are rare. Many that have occurred have been discovered as part of general incremental research activity, rather than as The Big Idea. Post-it notes, 3M's greatest claim to fame, were really a variation on a theme. The inventor of Post-its had been trying to invent a strong adhesive, and creatively explored the facets of the complete opposite – a very weak adhesive. The sweetener on which G. D. Searle's 'no aftertaste' Canderel is based was discovered accidentally, as a by-product of an experiment with proteins. It was the first food type to be granted a patent.

Even quantum leaps may require an extensive amount of work to realise their market opportunity, or they may be found to have less market potential than anticipated. A great many packs of Post-it notes were given away before they commanded the premium price they hold today. Canderel commands a high price because of its product advantages over other sweeteners and sugar, but it was still many years before product development costs were recouped. It still has to be heavily advertised on television. Fashionable young people were paid to walk around Tokyo with Sony Walkmans when they were first developed, in order to arouse interest in a product for which there was no apparent market!

Market testing is important, but it can fail, partly because those taking part in the test may lack imagination or because they may be too nice to be totally critical. It also fails to detect the 'inertia factor' which militates against new products. Product champions frequently say that they never realised how much time it would take before their idea started to be popular, and many entrepreneurs go out of business before the fruits of their new products are realised. Creativity exercises can provide some insight into prospective customer behaviour. Members of the team need to role-play customers and apply the 'so what?' test, introducing some hypothetical twists. It is likely that the team will want to repeat this several times during the product development life-cycle.

EXERCISE   TESTING MARKET OPPORTUNITY

> ■ Team members role-play customers. If the product is sold industry to industry, individual decision-makers in key customers can be the subjects of the role-play, or they might even attend in person! In the case of consumer products, the team must work with the psychographics (caricatures) of the segments who might buy the product.
> ■ The facilitator will pose the question to the team in role: 'XYZ PLC are introducing a new product which will help you with problem ABC. So what?'
> Repeat, with hypothetical twists: 'Despite the 20 per cent tax imposed on new products, XYZ PLC are introducing a new product which will help you with problem ABC. So what?' 'XYZ PLC are introducing a new product which will help you with problem ABC. If you take a free one now, they will give you £x to come back in three weeks with your opinion of it. So what?' 'XYZ PLC are introducing a new product which will help you with problem ABC and you will only be able to buy it from them by telephone. So what?'

Quantitative success

Profit potential is an essential consideration. The biggest challenge is to choose the right period of time, sensibly aligning profit expectations with the product's expected life-cycle. Professor Kay (quoted by Andrew Fisher in the *Financial Times*, 21/1/93) noted the tendency of some European firms to be good at innovations which proved to be not profitable enough to sustain success. There is also plenty of folklore about inventions initially unsuccessful in Britain which have been sold abroad and re-imported as successes. This phenomenon is attributed to British short-termism and hunger for quick returns. A broad understanding of profit potential is preferable; it can be seen as consisting of a variety of factors, including market share, achievement of qualitative objectives and providing an entrée to new markets.

Financial projections are subject to the same frailties as every human excursion into the future, with or without discounted cash flows and the capital asset pricing mechanism. Nevertheless, the power of spreadsheet software to facilitate speedy 'What if?' analysis is impressive and must be explored. One of the anecdotes I came across when I was gathering information for my first paper on creativity involved an accountant who was trying to help a client to avoid bankruptcy. He had used a spreadsheet package to model the customer's business and extrapolated a large number of variations on that customer's possible financial options in order to find a route out of their problems – and he succeeded. If spreadsheet 'What ifs' can provide that degree of benefit, how much more could 'What ifs' be applied to explore the profit potential of new products?

At the very least, a spreadsheet will be expected to indicate that the company can make a reasonable profit on a new product line if it reaches its target market at a price that market will bear. Also, of course, that profit will have to be made in a time-frame that the company's financial resources can bear.

Template   quantitative success – spreadsheet basics

	Year 1	Year 2	Year 3	Year 4	Year 5	Year 6
Volume						
Price						
Sales						
Direct costs						
Indirect costs						
Profit						

Ethics

Steve Cook has given some weight to environmental and ethical issues in his research. To the Co-operative Bank in the UK, ethical investment is the differential advantage which is advertised to attract new customers, and it has indeed been a factor in increasing the Bank's market share. However, companies do not have to be a Co-operative Bank or a Body Shop to be affected by ethical issues.

If a company bases its whole product advantage on ethics, then it runs the risk of presenting a 'holier than thou' stance which will attract the investigative zeal of a cynical press. That risk is nothing to the damage that the press could inflict on organisations which are sloppy about ethics. Newspaper headlines about large numbers of sales staff being suspended for selling inappropriate pensions, or directors of water companies who also hold directorates of companies involved in pollution do reach opinion formers. The worst unethical excesses of the business community, and public and voluntary organisations, end up in court.

Regular creativity exercises could be used to spot-check ethical issues. A truly progressive company would have a whistle-blowers' hotline to enable staff, customers or suppliers to report undesirable practices at every level. At the evaluation stage of idea-generation or problem-resolution the team concerned could play 'superachievers'. We have already discussed taking on the role of customers. This exercise involves individuals taking on the role of well-known characters, from St Francis of Assisi (the patron saint of animals) to Nelson Mandela, and even Goebbels (Hitler's propagandist) or Robert Maxwell.

EXERCISE SUPERACHIEVERS

Assume that the team have received early reports that the company's best-selling product may have some harmful side effects. Each team member must assume the role of a famous person, a recognisable superachiever, from history, literature or current news reports, saint or despot, and discuss the problem in role. Mother Theresa and Superman are favourite characters in these exercises, and a Margaret Thatcher is usually there to argue that there is no alternative to current policy. In the UK, Richard Branson and Anita Roddick are popular role models of ethical entrepreneurs, in the US, Ben and Jerry top the league. Business people with ruthless reputations would also have to be enrolled in order to balance the group.

Teams usually have a lot of fun in such an exercise at the same time as taking on board serious messages about the ethical and environmental implications of a product concept. There are examples of products where an 'ethical audit' might have saved the company concerned a lot of money in subsequent law suits. Most are in the high-risk area of pharmaceuticals, but faulty car design, toys, holidays to unbuilt hotels and aspects of government policies also spring to mind.

Resource constraints

The availability and synergy of resources are other vital aspects of the implementation of new product strategy. I have seen an enthusiastic new product development team brought to a despondent full stop when the availability of information technology resources to support a new product was pronounced 'zero'. There is an overall sizing exercise which should precede detailed project planning. Obviously, the resource requirement will have been costed at the financial evaluation stage. However, is it feasible that they can be made available?

A simple checklist will assist in this exercise – are the following available when and where they will be required?

- Funds
- People
- Skills
- Physical space
- Appropriate equipment
- Information
- Information systems support

A force field will be particularly helpful in addressing resource issues as shown in Figure 7.3.

Product developments do fail because of resource constraints. In this example, there are some very positive help factors, but a very big hindrance too and one which has delayed many projects. But, if a new product development can put an extra load on a computer system, which then triggers the need for a massive upgrade, there are probably another six managers around the company who are being held back on an information requirement because of that inhibitor. In the case of resource constraints, allies are very important. Multi-disciplinary teams not only provide an infinite variety of product champions, but provide a potential forum for solving common resource issues.

Having summarised the results of the force field analysis and perhaps having gathered a few allies outside the product development team, the next appropriate creativity exercise is the familiar

Figure 7.3 A force field applied to resource issues

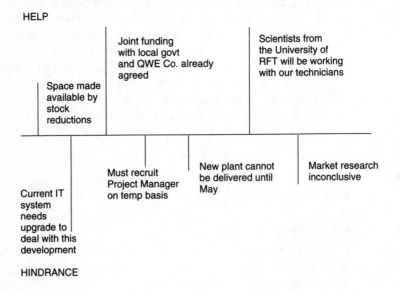

questioning technique. 'WHY–WHY?' and 'HOW–HOW?' discussions using the Fishbone diagram are obvious techniques for exploring resourcing. 'What if' scenarios, extreme or moderate, may also add important insights:

- What if our preferred supplier were wiped out by an earthquake?
- What if our top engineer started behaving badly? (Soichiro Honda was an inventive genius, but his behaviour was volatile. He was reputed to have rolled up to meetings with his bankers roaring drunk, to have seriously injured an employee, and he was implicated in the death of a geisha.)

Whenever I think about resourcing, I am reminded of the Ancient Mariner crying 'Water, water, everywhere, nor any drop to drink!' Resources have to be not only available but applicable. The analogy of the Ancient Mariner, cursed to be alone on his ship in a vast salty sea, dying of heat and thirst, might be familiar to many managers of ideas!

By exploring problems in advance, solutions can be found and/ or contingencies arranged. Project managers get an immense feeling of satisfaction when circumstances throw a spanner into the works and they have already got Plan B ready and waiting in their draw. Others believe that it only when there is a Plan B in the draw that any project has any hope of going according to plan!

Project planning

Before risks are assessed, project planning has to be undertaken. Large companies employ professional project managers equipped with sophisticated software to create project plans. They can define individual tasks in the project and their interdependencies to produce an optimum route to completion, or a number of suitable alternatives using the Programme Evaluation and Review Technique (PERT). For the manager who is not a project management professional but has to make sure that things get done, a GANTT chart which plots progress over time (see simple example below) would be an appropriate worksheet. I have also imposed the discipline of action working papers for individual team members (see example on p. 140) on a number of clients. The resentment born out of the tedium of completing them usually ensures that the actions are completed with a vengeance!

Example   GANTT chart

		Jun.	Jul.	Aug.	Sep.	Oct.	Nov.	Dec.	Jan.
CAD design	Plan	***	***						
	Actual	xxx	xxx	x					
Prototyping	Plan			***	***				
	Actual			xx	xxx				
Alpha test	Plan					***	***		
	Actual								
Beta test	Plan							***	***
	Actual								
Market test	Plan				***	***			
	Actual								
Pre-launch marketing	Plan								***
	Actual								

Template GANTT chart

		Jun.	Jul.	Aug.	Sep.	Oct.	Nov.	Dec.	Jan.
Design	Plan								
	Actual								
Prototyping	Plan								
	Actual								
Alpha test	Plan								
	Actual								
Beta test	Plan								
	Actual								
Market test	Plan								
	Actual								
Pre-launch marketing	Plan								
	Actual								

'The best-laid schemes o' mice and men gang oft awry', according to Robbie Burns, so why do we bother? We bother because planning can put individuals in control of their work and companies in control of markets. The more creative the planning, the more notable the success. Royal Dutch Shell were one of the weakest of the Seven Sisters in the early 1970s, the time of the oil crisis which shocked the whole industry. Shell realised that statistical extrapolations could tell them nothing about their business, which was so very dependent on geo-political trends. Shell is now famous for scenario planning, with several alternative plans for various parts of the world, and due in some part to that, Shell is now one of the more prosperous oil companies.

Research from a variety of sources indicates that planning and contingency planning make a positive contribution to company performance, and to employee performance, especially when 'why' is as prominent as 'how' in the distributed plan.

Example   project plan working paper

TEAM MEMBER: Hilary

OBJECTIVE/s:
Increase market share of nursery storage products by 10 per cent

STRATEGY:
Develop range of combination storage/entertainment products for the nursery

THIS PRODUCT:
Combination toy box/music box

BECAUSE:	**AND IF WE DON'T . . . ?**
Parents need help to persuade children to put away their toys	No known competition But, we need to keep impressing parents (and kids) with our innovations

What could go wrong?

Failure to launch in time for Christmas market

Contingency plan required?

Not applicable – time deadlines are sacrosanct EXCEPT IN CASE OF SAFETY ISSUES

ACTIONS:
(Therefore the following things need to be done . . .)

Overall project deadline: 31 July
Launch planned for: 1 September

Action 1:	Arrange 4 discussion groups with 12 new parents to examine prototypes	Action 2:	Arrange for parents to bring kids to play with prototypes
Deadline	28 Feb	Deadline	21 March
Budget?	£x,000	Budget?	£x,000
Action 3:	Commission creative agency for launch advertising	Action 4:	Visit major toy retailers
Deadline	30 April	Deadline	30 June
Budget?	£xx,000	Budget?	N/A

Template   project plan working paper

TEAM MEMBER:

OBJECTIVE/s:

STRATEGY:

THIS PRODUCT:

BECAUSE: **AND IF WE DON'T . . . ?**

What could go wrong?

Contingency plan required?

ACTIONS:
(Therefore the following things need to be done . . .)

Overall project deadline:
Launch planned for:

Action 1:   Action 2:

Deadline   Deadline
Budget?   Budget?

Action 3:   Action 4:

Deadline   Deadline
Budget?   Budget?

MARKETING RISKS

> He believed in the primacy of doubt, not as a blemish upon our ability to know, but as the essence of knowing.
>
> (James Gleick, biographer, speaking about Richard Feynman, Nobel prize winning physicist, 1992)

Steve Cook's model prompts for the assessment and reassessment of marketing and technical risks throughout product development. The following examples of marketing risks are taken primarily from articles by Mike Meldrum and Tony Millman (1991) of the Cranfield School of Management.

Cannibalisation

Dramatic product innovation often demands other dramatic actions, new subsidiary organisations, new alliances, new brand names or new routes to market.

It is almost inevitable that it will hasten the need for favoured cash cows to be ushered towards the abattoir. Many companies who have let their cash cows turn into sacred cows have paid a heavy price. It is one of those self-evident truths that if a company does not make its own products obsolete, someone else will. Cannibalisation can be managed more effectively when you are in charge of both the new product and the old.

Customer acceptance usually takes longer than forecast

Research conducted by Meldrum and Millman (1991) indicates that it is not uncommon for sales to take two to three times longer than anticipated even by industry experts to take off. In 1992 computer industry watchers were predicting that large numbers of organisations would downsize from mainframes to networked mini computers to reduce their IT costs. By 1994 this trend had not been realised. Even though many of those who had downsized were achieving cost reduction, others were reporting no significant cost reduction and others were concerned about the difficulties of managing data in a distributed environment. These factors, together with economic recession, encouraged the vast majority of mainframe users to stay put. In order to anticipate this risk, use reversal analysis. What if you were offering the exact opposite of this new product/service? Always practise reversal analysis on industry watchers' forecasts.

The cash flow implications of slow customer take-up are obvious. New businesses usually underestimate the time it will take to establish their products or services, and this is one reason why so many fail in the first two years of operation. The same problem can scupper good new products from established firms. Spreadsheet 'What ifs? can help to manage this risk.

Customer mismanagement of the product/service

Customer service experts now suggest that good service means not just putting right your own mistakes, but those of the customer as well. If customers make poor use of your innovation, the market will be poisoned. Excessive attention to detail during alpha and beta testing should ensure that potential misuse is anticipated and the appropriate level of service provided with the product.

Years ago, a couched expression of 'read the manual' was a common response from telephone enquiry lines for technical products, even when the customer was paying an annual service fee and for the telephone call. Today, even commodity food items, like margarine, carry freephone numbers to enable customers to make enquiries about recipes and calories.

Role-playing, and 'in their shoes' scenarios will raise the team's sensitivity to alternative perceptions of the product and also to alternative interpretations of instructions in the manual or on the packet. Remember physicist's Richard Feynman's approach to experiments – 'If I were an electron – what would I do?' Qualitative market research is also desirable. One own-label food manufacturer conducted a 'So what' examination of food labelling and discovered that information on fat and fibre content meant little to consumers. They changed their labelling from exact proportions to high/medium/low, so that consumers could make an informed purchase rather than a confused one.

Being late to market

It happened to Tower Bridge long before Concorde and the Channel Tunnel. This frequent problem is usually caused by a mismatch of resources, which even hardened planners have a tendency to underestimate in cases of the greatest technical challenges. However much work is done up front, things change and the application of plant, money and skills to the project can be skewed. The other side of this coin is the high-tech companies who have so feared being late to market that they have launched inadequately tested products. 'Murder-boarding' can help the team to cast the worst possible light on the plan and make allowances for what could go wrong.

Lack of infrastructure

A concept may precede available technology by many years. Popular science fiction provides many examples – the TV series *Thunderbirds* featured video phones 30 years before they were widely available. The telephonic infrastructure of the 1960s could not have supported video phones, but somehow we always knew that one day they would be on sale. Meldrum and Millman (1991) give the example of the paperless office, which was promoted as a concept before scanning and storage technology had reached a stage which could support it. Such product concepts have to bide their time. Hyping something which cannot yet be realised must be handled as a very long-term PR campaign as much as an issue of product development.

Timing of the patent

In addition to Meldrum and Millman's (1991) considerations, timing of the patent application for a new product is a factor in marketing risk. A patent gives the patentee a useful monopoly to make, use or sell the invention for a fixed period of time (up to a maximum of 20 years in Britain). The Patent Office in the UK also deals with the registration of industrial designs and the registration of trade marks. Design registration offers five years' protection which can be renewed for 25 years. Trade mark protection lasts initially for seven years and can be renewed indefinitely. A branch of The Patent Office deals with intellectual property and copyright.

However, as the Patent Office (HMSO, 1989) say themselves in their booklet: 'Many firms use patent specifications to find out what their competitors are up to – what research they are carrying out or what products they are about to launch.' Consequently, some companies, such as an electrical products firm who were introducing a new cabling casing product, take the risk of postponing patent registration until just before product launch, especially if their concept might be easily copied.

Copying is one of the most serious marketing risks. Illegal copyists will not be deterred by the law. Even reputable firms can be quite determined to push their luck.

In May 1994, Yves Saint-Laurent successfully sued rival Ralph Lauren for copying one of its 1970 dress designs, a black tuxedo dress, in 1992. Yves Saint-Laurent spend FF50m per annum fighting counterfeiting, Chanel spend FF30m. Usually, cases involve the 'knock-off merchants', copyists at the lower end of the fashion business. This was the first case involving two prestigious names (*Financial Times*)

Imitation is indeed the sincerest form of flattery, and companies have to assume that if their product really is the best then copying is bound to happen. It is prudent to put money aside to pay for legal injunctions and rewards for people reporting illegal copying. The sort of advertising that establishes their overwhelming brand dominance is also expensive. However, prevention is always better than cure.

When even the masterpieces of Renaissance artists can be copied, what on earth can companies do to prevent illegal copying? *Every creativity technique should be applied in the pursuit of solutions, and analogy may be quite successful.* For example, how do dogs distinguish their owner from their owner's twin? – by smell! What techniques are used to detect counterfeit currency, etc.?

As for legitimate copying after a patent has expired, the only protection is to have moved on to patent the next generation of the product.

Customer loyalty

Is the customer group you want to buy your new product actively discontented with what they have at the moment? Old technologies and old services sometimes take a long time to die. There is a massive price differential between milk delivered in pint bottles to domestic doorsteps by warm human beings and the cheaper option of lugging milk in huge containers round a supermarket and queuing to pay for it. Yet, the traditional milk delivery service endures.

In computer software, the old adage that 'if it ain't broke, don't fix it!' is also enduring. 'Legacy' systems (computerspeak for 1960s' technology) survive because they go on producing desired results.

Customer loyalty is not necessarily a reason for failing to initiate change, but it does affect the size of the accessible market for a new product. 'In their shoes' (as well as market research) may help the project team to assess how strongly customers feel about their relationship with the currently available solution.

TECHNICAL RISKS

The product proves to be inadequate

The most common cause of inadequacy is likely to be that the product or service is not of a high enough quality to meet customer expectations. I have heard senior managers who ought to know better declare that marketing can compensate for a weak product. *It can't.*

The product proves to be too complex

The most common cause of quality problems is over-complexity. 'Murder-boarding' to identify the potential for de-engineering will also help to minimise this risk and to 'keep it simple, stupid (KISS)'. Especially when a product is introduced, it ought not to need lots of bells and whistles. It ought to have one overridingly clear advantage over what has gone before. Even with services, such as savings accounts, customers can be confused by too many features, and be consequently hesitant. Meanwhile, there is money being wasted in the administration of these features.

The mysteries of industry standards

It is a mystery why VHS home videos prevailed as a standard over Betamax, the supposedly better product. It is a mystery why the esoteric and academic UNIX operating system became a standard in the computer industry. It is a mystery why the menus of so many Indian restaurants seem to be so similar when the cuisine of the whole sub-continent is hugely varied. No matter what emerges as 'the standard', we can only be sure that consumers like standards.

Unfortunately, in the world of technology, this sometimes means that manufacturers have to back two horses until one or other emerges as 'the standard'. Sometimes, the significant minority interest will survive, like Apple in a PC world dominated by Microsoft Windows.

A creative approach to minimising this type of risk is to share it with companies who have a mutual strategic interest in the outcome. Supplier-customer partnerships, introduced by the Japanese, are now common in Europe. I have also come across two suppliers and a mutual customer researching together to produce a cleaner manufacturing process. Many high-tech companies, in order to maintain the pace of innovation, collaborate with competitors in order to ensure that any result of joint research can become a new standard and costs can be reduced.

Summary checklist

In the following example, the positive factors about new product X are weighed up against the risks. The importance of each factor is weighted, and weightings may vary from company to company and from product line to product line. Scores are assigned, up to a maximum of 10, which indicates the most positive or most negative. When the scores are added up, the size of surplus or deficit gives an indication of how favourable a prospect this new product development is. This provides a simple and quick summary of the ground covered. Assigning numbers to subjective judgements is a matter of spurious accuracy and the results should never be treated as sacrosanct. However, they are as good as many numbers put into serious forecasts! Using a numerical 'tag' ensures that each item is properly considered and a degree of likely success (or otherwise) is deduced.

Product X, in the example, achieves a healthy surplus of positive over negative factors. In fact, the success scores outweigh the risks by almost 4:1. Detailed analysis suggests that contingency plans would be needed in some areas – especially ensuring resource availability and ensuring compliance with industry standards. Special attention is also required to ensure a timely market entry and to accelerate customer acceptance. Reviewers might also be concerned about the modest score on profit potential, given that it bears the highest weighting of the success factors. However, noting that the product looks a relatively low risk, it is not surprising that it might only offer middling returns, and this may be acceptable in the balance of the company's product portfolio.

Example issues, risks – summary checklist

(weightings are a percentage, scores: 10 = highest, 1 = lowest)

Factor	weight	score	weight x score
POSITIVE:			
Product's synergy with corporate culture	12	6	72
Product advantage	18	7	126
Market opportunity	18	6	108
Quantitative success – profit potential	20	5	100
Ethics	7	10	70
Resource availability	10	4	40
Project planning	15	7	105
POSITIVE FACTOR RATING	100		621
NEGATIVE:			
Marketing risks:			
cannibalisation control	12	5	60
speed of customer acceptance	7	7	49
ability to avoid misuse	15	3	45
timely market entry	15	7	105
infrastructure in place	5	1	5
timing of patent	5	2	10
ability to overcome inertia factors	7	5	35
Technical risks:			
adequacy of product	20	2	40
industry standards	14	8	112
NEGATIVE FACTOR RATING	100		461
TOTAL			160

Template   issues, risks – summary checklist

(weightings are a percentage, scores: 10 = highest, 1 = lowest)

Factor	weight	score	weight x score
POSITIVE:			
Product's synergy with corporate culture			
Product advantage			
Market opportunity			
Quantitative success – profit potential			
Ethics			
Resource availability			
Project planning			
POSITIVE FACTOR RATING			
NEGATIVE:			
Marketing risks:			
cannibalisation control			
speed of customer acceptance			
ability to avoid misuse			
timely market entry			
infrastructure in place			
timing of patent			
ability to overcome inertia factors			
Technical risks:			
adequacy of product			
industry standards			
NEGATIVE FACTOR RATING			
TOTAL			

products are there to be explored, but also to be ..orge Bernard Shaw declared that all progress comes ..asonable man, and we would be in a sorry state if all ..starting with the wheel had been subject to analysis ..Nevertheless, if the boldness of the hero does not consist ..ing directly against the nature of things, extensive testing .. ..nning must be put in place to ensure that understanding of the nature of things supports the organisation's creative endeavours.

In itself, the whole implementation workshop is a 'murder-boarding' of the product concept. Divergent thinking does not always have to be positive. There is a time and place for putting new product concepts through creative criticism, and it has to be before commitment of production funding. Product failures cannot be precluded altogether, but minimising them is as good for morale as encouraging creativity in the first place. Teams working on the next project for the future want to produce a success just as much as they want to have freedom to explore the widest variety of possible innovations.

CONCLUSION

Trade is almost as old as humanity itself. Stone Age people discovered that their comfort was improved by exchanging their knives for other tribes' pots, and beads for spices. Members of any product development team should keep their Palaeolithic ancestors in mind. They had to present their knives to their prospects, let them feel them and test them. The prospect's very survival might depend on the knife. If it failed to perform its essential function, the two tribes might end up going to war. If its cutting performance was good, the tribes would become allies, inter-marry and secure a future generation. Products really mattered.

This book has revisited the importance of product, starting with perfecting the core function to fulfil someone's need. We have clothed that core with measurable services and positive intangible attributes. We have varied the product. We have explored the intangible attributes of the marketing mix. We have also looked at the challenges and risks inherent in bringing products to market. The purpose of the book has been to introduce techniques to generate large quantities of ideas about every aspect of product.

If the sum total of the world's inspired products is increased by even one as a result of it, the effort was worthwhile!

— *Bibliography and further reading*

The majority of examples and references in this book are drawn from popular articles which have appeared in the press between 1991–1995. The *Financial Times* has provided most, followed by the *Sunday Times*, *Business Week*, the *Daily Mirror*, the *Director*, *Marketing Business* and the *Journal of Creative Behavior*.

For those wishing to explore further some of the areas touched upon in this book, the following books and articles could be useful:

Berry, Zeithaml and Parasuraman, 1990, 'Five Imperatives for Improving Service Quality', *Sloan Management Review*.

Bowman, Cliff, 1990, *The Essence of Strategic Management*, Hemel Hempstead, Prentice Hall.

Burns, Tom, 1961, *The Management of Innovation*, Oxford, Oxford University Press.

Christopher, Martin and McDonald, Malcolm, 1985, *Effective Marketing Management*, Buckinghamshire, Open University Press.

von Clausewitz, Carl, 1832, *On War*.

Cook, Steve, 1994, *New Product Manager* (software product), Cranfield School of Management.

Cooper, R. G. and Kleinschmidt, E. J., 1987 'Success Factors in

Product Innovation', *Industrial Marketing Management*, Vol. 16.

Davis, Stanley, 1987, *Future Perfect*, Reading, MA, Addison-Wesley.

De Bono, Edward, 1990, *I am Right/You are Wrong*, New York, Viking.

Edwards Deming, W., 1982, *Quality, Productivity and Competitive Position*, Cambridge, MA, Center for Advanced Engineering Study.

Garvin, David A., 1984, 'What Does Quality really Mean?', *Sloan Management Review*, Fall, pp. 29–30.

Grossman, Stephen R., 1994, 'Transcendence as a Subset of Evolutionary Thinking: A Darwinian View of the Creative Experience', *Journal of Creative Behavior*, Vol. 28, No. 4.

Handy, Charles, 1994, *The Empty Raincoat*, London, Hutchinson.

Harvey-Jones, Sir John, 1990, *Making it Happen*, London, Collins.

Janis, Irving L., 1971, 'Groupthink', *Psychology Today*, November.

Kearns, D. T. and Nadler, D. A., 1992, *Prophets in the Dark*, New York, Harper Business.

Larson, Cynthia M. for Narrative Strategies, 1993, 'Bridging the Innovation Gap – An Interview with Robert Johnson', *Journal of Creative Behavior*, Vol. 27, No. 2.

McDonald, Denison, Ryals, Rogers and Yallop, 1994, *Marketing: The Challenge of Change*, London, Chartered Institute of Marketing.

Majaro, Simon, 1992, *Managing Ideas for Profit*, McGraw Hill.

Mattimore, B. W., 1994, *99% Inspiration*, New York, American Management Association (Amacom).

Meldrum, M. J. and Millman, A. F., 1991, 'Ten Risks in Marketing High-technology Products', *Industrial Marketing Management*.

Miller, William C., 1987, *The Creative Edge*, Reading, MA, Addison-Wesley.

Morgan, Gareth, 1993, *Immaginization*, London, Sage.

Morita, Akio with Edwin M. Rheingold and Mitsuko Shimomura, 1987, *Made in Japan*, New York, Collins.

van Oech, Roger, 1983, *A Whack on the Side of the Head*, Warner.

Peters, Tom, 1989, *Thriving on Chaos*, London, Pan.

Pfeffer, Jeffrey, 1994, *Competitive Advantage through People*, Boston, MA, Harvard Business School Press.

Proctor, R. A., 1989, 'The Use of Metaphors to Aid the Process of Creative Problem Solving', *Personnel Review*, Vol. 18, No. 4, pp. 33–42.

Schonberger and Knod, 1991, *Operations Management – Improving Customer Service*, Irwin.

Senge, Peter M., 1990, *The Fifth Discipline*, New York, Doubleday.

UK Patent Office, 1989, *The Patent Office*, London, HMSO.

Utterback, James, 1994, *Mastering the Dynamics of Innovation*, Boston, MA, Harvard Business School Press.

Van Gundy, Arthur B., 1984, *Managing Group Creativity*, New York, American Management Association (Amacom).

Wernick, Robert, 1993, 'Murder by Bureaucracy', *Reader's Digest*, January.